So You Want To Be Used By God?

How to Operate in the Supernatural & the Gifts of the Spirit

Stephen & Shirley Carson

Copyright © 2005
By
Stephen Carson
Shirley Carson, D.R.E.

All rights reserved. No part of this book may be reproduced in any form except for the inclusion of brief quotations in a review, without permission in writing from the author or publisher.

ISBN:978-0-9742382-3-4

Printed in the United States by
Morris Publishing
3212 East Highway 30
Kearney, NE. 68847
1-800-650-7888

Table of Contents

Introduction..

Part 1 - How To Be Used By God

    Chapter One - Prayer..3

    Chapter Two - Spiritual Warfare......................11

    Chapter Three - Gifts of the Spirit.....................31

    Chapter Four - Fear of Failure........................63

Part 2 - How To Keep The Anointing

    Chapter Five - A Servants Heart......................79

    Chapter Six - You Must Pass The Test..............91

    Chapter Seven - Contagious............................103

Bibliography..113

Introduction

So, you want to be used by God. Being used by God is an awesome privilege, which should not be taken lightly. There are many that say they want to be used by God, but they have no idea how to begin. We felt lead of the Lord to write a guide that will help start you on your journey. If you have already begun the trip, then we pray this book will help you to refocus your vision and calling. This book will be split into 2 parts. The first part will focus on how to be used by God and the Gifts of the Spirit. The second part of this book will focus on how to maintain and keep the anointing flowing in your life.

In business school they taught me that in order to start a business there were things that needed to be considered before you actually start the business. Being used by God is serious business; therefore there are things that also must be considered. The work of God is not something you just jump into without giving it any thought. God's business must be entered with much prayer. The work of God is multi-faceted, and one must know which area God has called them into. All of us have different gifts and talents; therefore we must find the ministry where these gifts and talents can be the most beneficial.

Just because you know how to cook BBQ chicken, doesn't mean you need to open up a chicken restaurant. You may be able to cook, but not be able to manage. You must know your gifting and then be confident enough to stay within the parameters of those giftings. That being said, we must understand that the cook and the manager are just as important.
They are on the same team and without each other the business would fail.

God's business is the same way, and we all have a role to play. My role is no more important than your role. One of the things that have hindered the work of God is the mistake of thinking a particular role is of little importance. It does not matter what area God has called you into, that area is important.

This book will not give you a specific formula describing the prophetic call and the way you hear the voice of God. God's methods are unique. However, I hope to give you some signposts to follow. One thing I have learned through the years is that not all prophetic calls are alike. Each person is unique in his or her gifts and abilities. The ways of God kneaded into our lives have molded each of us in a different fashion.

Stay where God called you. Be proud of your calling. Commit yourself to your calling. God will use you to do great things for His kingdom. And remember if God called you, and He has called all of us, the calling He has placed on our life is of the utmost importance.

Part 1:

How To Be Used By God

Chapter One

Prayer – The Real Key

Prayer; what is this thing we often say we do but seldom enjoy? Prayer is the conduit which translates us from our own way of living and ushers us into the realm of his presence. Prayer kills this flesh we love to protect and nurture. Prayer helps me die to myself and yield myself to the Master. Prayer is something that has become useless and boring in the eyes of many Christians. Is it because we seldom hear the master speak back? Is it because we don't get the answers we petition Him about? Or is it because we are not in control while we are participating in it? Prayer is something we do unto God which brings us closer to Him.

I can remember when I was young growing up in our church. Bishop L.A. Parent was the presiding Pastor over our congregation and he was a powerful man of God. Prayer was not just something he taught us. Prayer was who he was. Because of his prayer life, he was well known as a prophet in his own time. He was a man that looked you in the eye and saw all the way to the sole of your feet. When you got around Bishop L.A. Parent, you knew He had been with the Lord.

Bishop taught me tremendous things growing up. When there were problems in the church, I can remember him calling a church meeting. Church members of every age were expected to be there. Parents brought their little ones with their blankets, pillows and bottles, and we stayed and prayed until we either heard from God or the problem got fixed. Yes, I know what you are thinking. It doesn't take all that. But my question is real. Doesn't it? Our church was one of apostolic ministry. Many great things happened amongst the people of God. There was little fornication or hidden sin that lingered in the church because the eyes of the prophetic was very sharp.

All these things taught me that prayer played an important role in being used by God. Now that I am grown, I am raising a family of my own; God has once again proved to me that it still takes all that and a little bit more. Prayer is the one thing we are lacking the most. I know that prayer can seem boring, but it is only boring in the sense we do not enjoy whom we are spending time with. There is a danger in being so busy working for the

Lord that we never spend the quality time needed in prayer to go to that next level in Him.

What I like about prayer is you can't fake prayer. It is either in your heart or it's not. But because we can't see a man's heart like God does, we come and pray with things in our spirit and we never try to fix them. Therefore, prayer becomes more work than pleasure. I have found that those with a pure heart and a right spirit often enjoy their prayer time. Prayer is not drudgery. Prayer is another invitation to spend time with the greatest person I know. Jesus.

We have been preaching for Rev. Jeff Arnold and I enjoyed spending good quality time with him. He is a man of great passion and faith. I thought how interesting it was to watch certain people try to gain an audience with him just to spend time with him, to hear what he had to say. Why? Because he is a powerful person who has great insight and his rich company is always a pleasure to grace. But how much more should we want to spend time with the one true God. The one who breathed life into us? The one who woke me up this morning, took care of my wants and needs?

We make prayer too much a drudgery. Prayer is not drudgery. I enjoy spending time with the one who takes care of me. As I married into the ministry and watched the prayer life of my husband, I was amazed at how much time he spent with the Lord. I have to tell you at first I thought he was a little off his rocker. I would watch him pray and sway back and forth. I thought "boy is he a strange one." But little did I know he was in intimate relationship with God.

Many want the Gifts of the Spirit without paying the cost. This will not happen. This is what makes some people angry. It is easy to swindle people in life to get what we want, when we want it. But we are on God's terms and when it comes to God, that doesn't work. You can't talk God into doing something for you that you don't deserve. THAT makes some of us mad because we want to do the things He did without paying the cost ourselves.

Just when you thought everyone else was being blessed and getting away with murder, when it comes to God, no one is getting away with anything. God knows it all.

This is why I want to talk to you about one of the most important keys to being used by God. It's called Prayer. We have got to get back to the basics of an intimate relationship with God. This is the missing link in why we are failing at being used by Him. Am I saying we will never fail if we pray? No. But I am saying we have a big Father backing us up when we pray. You can walk through life with boldness knowing you have a rich heritage with the Lord.

I have many friends who feel like excess prayer is a works mentality. Prayer is not a works mentality. Prayer is the thing that kills out this flesh and makes me submit myself to a deeper dimension so I may walk and be used like He did while He was here on this earth. Prayer is the portal that opens communication between me and the Lord. When that portal is open, everything He says can be heard. This is a powerful thing. God is always speaking. The problem is we are not always listening.

My husband and I strongly believe in our prayer lives. When we don't pray, we feel the effects of it. The same thing applies when you don't eat right. Your body feels the effect of it. So prayer is something that cannot be neglected.

My husband was frustrated one day and asked the Lord why His voice seemed so faint and why he wasn't hearing the Lord as clear. God's reply was, "I haven't gone anywhere. You are the one that has moved away from my lips." When we stopped and realized what had happened, we had gotten so busy, that our prayer life was suffering. Were we still praying? Yes, but not like we should. As a result of that our ministry became sluggish, while the whole time we were wondering where God was. And God was asking "Where are you?"

Prayer is not something we do. Prayer is who we are. A prayer less person is like a wire with no electrical flow. It's dead. It still may have a little juice, but eventually, that will subside. I watch many people receive an impartation of the Gifts of the Spirit through consistent, rich, prayer, only to retreat away once they receive the gift. Does the gift still work? Yes. But ask Moses what happened when the gift still worked. Because of his disobedience in staying close to the Master's side, he was judged and refused from entering into the promise land. It may look like you are getting away with your lack of prayer, but understand one thing. God keeps good books. He is not like you and I who are slack in our understanding. He knows. You may still operate in the spirit for a while, but there is a great fall that is coming if you don't return to old fashion prayer. I have watched many people be mightily used by God, and lose it all because they lost their connection in prayer. I watch men and women run themselves incessantly in the ministry and they think they are getting away with no repercussions in their body. At least for now they do. But in the end it always catches up with them and manifests in their physical bodies. Ask Jezebel. She thought she could do things wrong and thought she was getting away for years without God judging. But one day the horses came trotting by and her time was up and she had to pay the pauper. You see, one way or the other, we pay for what we do and for what we don't do. Prayer is something we can't afford not to do.

I have many people ask us, "what do you say when you pray? How long do you have to pray to get where you are?" Well, for one thing, when I pray I talk to God just as if He were sitting there. God hates to be addressed as if He was some third person in the trinity. Many people talk to God like he is in the third person. I talk to God just as if I was talking to a friend on the phone. I tell Him things that make me mad. I talk to him about people who disappoint me and the things that eat away at my very being. I talk to Him about how I don't understand where He is and why it seems like He is not coming through for me. <u>I am very candid when I pray.</u> That is why I believe everyone needs a prayer closet where no one is around and no one can hear. That way I am able to be open and honest with Him. You won't believe this, but God loves it when we pour ourselves out to Him. He loves our company.

When I backslid and came back to the Lord I had a lot of issues and dysfunctions that had to be healed. In one of many prayer sessions with the Lord I received a great deliverance. It was after this that I realized this prayer thing was real and it worked. When He touched me in a way I had never been touched, it drew me very close to His side. I learned He is a person with feelings just like I am. When I started to develop a rich prayer life, it was like reading a mystery novel. There were all kinds of corners and turns that bore great excitement. It became an adventure. This is when prayer becomes fun. But this kind of prayer only comes from being consistent.

When I pray I often envision myself pressing up against His chest and trying to hear His heartbeat. I know that probably sounds crazy. But I am on a mission to know how He feels and what He thinks. It is this closeness that attracts God's presence to us. It is this hunger to know Him that brings great anointing and revelation. Some of the greatest revelations I ever received were from spending intimate time with the Master. God knows when I'm praying and if my heart and mind are really there or not.

One way I know if people are really prayer warriors is by the fruit they bare. It has nothing to do with judging. There is only one judge. But it doesn't take a scientist to look at a piece of fruit and tell you what it is. That is how God helps us to be able to tell the difference between those who pray and those who just look like they are praying. Real prayer bleeds all the way through the spirit to the soul and then to the flesh. It is an inward expression that makes its way to the outside. Those who really pray have an inner work of the Holy Ghost. You can't fake that.

Watchman Nee wrote some awesome things in his book "The Spiritual Man" that taught me a lot. He taught very heavily on body, soul and spirit. This is something that is seldom taught in our churches. But it is something that Paul taught in the scriptures.

1 Thessalonians 5:23 says, "And the very God of peace sanctify you wholly; and I pray God your whole <u>spirit</u> and <u>soul</u> and <u>body</u> be preserved blameless unto the coming of our Lord Jesus Christ."

There is a place in prayer, as we spend more quality time with Him, our pureness bleeds through our spirit to our soul and then to our flesh, which can lead to great deliverance in personality flaws and physical healings. Prayer is such a powerful thing. We have only begun to scratch the surface of the powerful things that can be accomplished in prayer.

If you don't have a prayer life, start today. If you do have a prayer life and your prayer life is lacking, take some time and recommit to prayer. Prayer makes the difference and prayer is the main key to being used by God. I know that some of you are frustrated with hearing that prayer is the main key to being used by God and hearing His voice. but I tell you, it is the truth. We must return back to our enriched prayer time with God and I guarantee you, <u>if you commune with Him, He will show up and show out in your life.</u>

Chapter Two

Spiritual Warfare

Spiritual Warfare is a very important thing in the life of a believer. If you are going to be successful at fighting your adversary, the devil, you are going to have to learn how to beat him at his own game.

We know the scripture let's us know that we are more than conquerors through Christ Jesus. There is no reason not to win every fight against our adversary.

Ephesians 6:10-18 tells us;

> "Finally, my brethren, be strong in the Lord, and in the power of his might.
>
> Put on the whole armour of God, that ye may be able to stand against the wiles of the devil.
>
> For we wrestle not against flesh and blood, but against principalities, against powers, against the rulers of the darkness of this world, against spiritual wickedness in high places.
>
> Wherefore take unto you the whole armour of God, that ye may be able to withstand in the evil day, and having done all, to stand.
>
> Stand therefore, having your loins girt about with truth, and having on the breastplate of righteousness;
>
> And your feet shod with the preparation of the gospel of peace;
>
> Above all, taking the shield of faith, wherewith ye shall be able to quench all the fiery darts of the wicked.
>
> And take the helmet of salvation, and the sword of the Spirit, which is the word of God:

Praying always with all prayer and supplication in the Spirit, and watching thereunto with all perseverance and supplication for all saints;"

You see, Christ not only told us we would win, He also told us HOW to win. I can remember buying our son a bike for Christmas one year. The bicycle came with a manual on how to successfully assemble it. If we followed the manual, the bike worked properly. If we didn't follow the manual (which my dad always thought he could do without!) the bike often made a strange noise.

Christ gave us His Word for a reason and He had a purpose in mind. It is the only thing that truly defeats the enemy.

Ephesians tells us to put on the whole armor of God. It is vital to understand the importance of putting on the whole armor of God. This is the very first thing the Word tells us to do. Before you fight any battle, make sure you have on the right clothing.

The next thing Ephesians tells us is that we wrestle not against flesh and blood. In other words, never forget what we are wrestling against is spiritual, not fleshly. If you ever forget that principal, you lose your footing in the battle.

The last thing it tells us to do is pray always. In other words, before you war and after you are through fighting, don't forget to pray. Prayer is the glue that holds everything together. Prayer is the key ingredient.

Every war a born-again believer fights is Spiritual.

II Corinthians 10:3-5 reads;

> "For though we walk in the flesh, we do not war after the flesh: (For the weapons of our warfare are not carnal, but mighty through God to the pulling down of strong holds;)
>
> Casting down imaginations, and every high thing that exalteth itself against the knowledge of God, and bringing into captivity every thought to the obedience of Christ;"

The mind is a powerful thing. It is one of the only things the enemy uses as a tool against our lives. This is where the demonic realm tries to manifest itself.

Let me give you a powerful example of how the enemy will use our minds and the minds of others to work his purpose.

Job 2:2-9 states;

> "And the LORD said unto Satan, From whence comest thou? And Satan answered the LORD, and said, From going to and fro in the earth, and from walking up and down in it.
>
> And the LORD said unto Satan, Hast thou considered my servant Job, that there is none like him in the earth, a perfect and an upright man, one that feareth God, and escheweth evil? and still he holdeth fast his integrity, although thou

movedst me against him, to destroy him without cause.

And Satan answered the LORD, and said, Skin for skin, yea, all that a man hath will he give for his life.

But put forth thine hand now, and touch his bone and his flesh, and he will curse thee to thy face.

And the LORD said unto Satan, Behold, he is in thine hand; but save his life.

So went Satan forth from the presence of the LORD, and smote Job with sore boils from the sole of his foot unto his crown.

And he took him a potsherd to scrape himself withal; and he sat down among the ashes.

Then said his wife unto him, Dost thou still retain thine integrity? curse God, and die."

The accusation the enemy went to God with to condemn Job didn't work. Job did not believe the lie. Next we find the enemy using Job's wife.

I have to stop and tell you that the enemy often uses people that are the closest to us. I do not feel people say these things of their own accord. They are thoughts that are injected in the mind of a believer, and unless the believer is spirit controlled, those thoughts from the enemy are blurted out in a crucial time that can cause much hurt.

That's why to gain surpassing victory in this life you must keep your mind on the right things and bring every thought into the knowledge of God.

Philippians 4:8-9 tells us;

> "Finally, brethren, whatsoever things are true, whatsoever things are honest, whatsoever things are just, whatsoever things are pure, whatsoever things are lovely, whatsoever things are of good report; if there be any virtue, and if there be any praise, think on these things.
>
> Those things, which ye have both learned, and received, and heard, and seen in me, do: and the God of peace shall be with you."

Anything that tears down, steals, kills, or destroys is not from the Lord. This is how we rightfully judge every thought.

II Corinthians 2:11 reads, "For we are not ignorant of his devices."

We are to study the manual He has given us in order to fight this battle and be strategic. What God is really saying is, "you have no excuse to lose this battle." He has given us everything we need to, not just conqueror the battle, but to win the war!

Ephesians 4:27 tells us, "Neither give place to the devil." It is important that you stand your ground in this fight of Faith. The way you lose ground is by giving in to fear. Fear is Faith in reverse. Fear is Faith in the enemy. That is why it is vitally important you stand your ground.

Luke 10:19-20 lets us know what Christ left us in the Spirit;

> "Behold, I give unto you power to tread on serpents and scorpions, and over all the power of the enemy: and nothing shall by any means hurt you.
>
> Notwithstanding in this rejoice not, that the spirits are subject unto you; but rather rejoice, because your names are written in heaven."

Despite what some of you are thinking, Christ did not leave us powerless. You can't mistake delay for failure. Just because we go through struggles doesn't mean we have failed or Christ has failed us. Therefore, this leads me to this next question. Some of you are asking, "Why am I not getting victory when I pray?"

Can I tell you, you are? It's just the answer is being held up in the spirit realm. Some of you feel like your prayers aren't getting off the floor, but they are. What is really happening is the answer is being held up in the spirit realm. Here is a great example of an answer being delayed.

Daniel 10:11-13 ministers so powerfully;

> "And he said unto me, O Daniel, a man greatly beloved, understand the words that I speak unto thee, and stand upright: for unto thee am I now sent. And when he had spoken this word unto me, I stood trembling.
>
> Then said he unto me, Fear not, Daniel: for from the first day that thou didst set thine heart to understand, and to chasten thyself before thy God, thy words were heard, and I am come for thy words.
>
> But the prince of the kingdom of Persia withstood me one and twenty days: but, lo, Michael, one of the chief princes, came to help me; and I remained there with the kings of Persia."

Some of you feel like you were doing well and all of a sudden you felt like an attack from the enemy came out of nowhere.

You have to be careful because there are spirits that can attach themselves to you through people or places.

Here is a great example in Acts 16:16-18;

> "And it came to pass, as we went to prayer, a certain damsel possessed with a spirit of

divination met us, which brought her masters much gain by soothsaying:

The same followed Paul and us, and cried, saying, These men are the servants of the most high God, which shew unto us the way of salvation.

And this did she many days. But Paul, being grieved, turned and said to the spirit, I command thee in the name of Jesus Christ to come out of her. And he came out the same hour."

These spirits are called "Tracking Spirits". We sometimes pick up these spirits from being somewhere or coming into contact with a certain individual.

John G. Lake said he was at a prayer meeting one day very sick. A man asked if he could pray for Him and he said yes. After the man prayed for him he wrestled for 3 days with sexual and perverse thoughts. Later he found out that this man was into pornography and the spirit he had attached itself to him. It was tracking him.

That's why I don't let just anyone lay hands on me. As a matter of fact, I'm particular who I let lay hands on me. Don't let that make you feel bad. You've got to protect yourself. If you don't protect yourself, no one else will.

Another way you can pick up on spirits is in your dreams. This is when the body is at its most neutral point.

Dreaming is your spirit and the spirit realm connecting together. It is picking up on things around you.

That's how you can have homosexual thoughts, thoughts of perversion, violence, adultery and any other form of sin because you are picking up on what is going on in the spirit realm around you.

The enemy will even let you dream things that include yourself partaking in them, hoping you will buy into the lie and make you believe you have a particular problem or struggle. When in actuality, you have no struggle; they are just induced thoughts in the nighttime.

Dreaming is like standing out in the sun on a sunny day and saying, "boy it sure is hot out." We don't feel bad for feeling the heat of the sun. Neither should you feel bad for feeling the heat of the spiritual realm in your dreams. You are only picking up on what is around you or what is around you in your city.

They are NOT YOUR THOUGHTS.

This is where people mess up and fall into sin. They think they are bad people for dreaming these things. They are not your dreams. You have to be able to distinguish that; if you don't, you will be terribly deceived.

There are also times when people may be talking about you or praying against you. This type of spiritual activity is felt very much in the spirit realm. That is why we cover ourselves with prayer and we also are responsible by not talking about our brother.

You may be asking "Why did God choose me?" I did too. Some people are anointed for spiritual warfare. These people are usually those who have been through a lot of trials or tragedies.

For some reason the anointing is attracted to trouble. There is something about trouble that produces a greater anointing. Do I like it? No, but His ways are higher than my ways. They are past finding out. As long as I know I am in the palm of His hands, I know no one can pluck me out or destroy me. That makes going through troubled times a little easier.

Some of you may be asking "Why am I fighting the same Spirit? I thought I whipped this spirit?"

Francis Frangipane wrote an article entitled, "GOLIATH HAD A BROTHER." I would like to share this article with you. It is very powerful.

"Here's the scene: You're in a battle with sickness, oppression or some similar need. However, you seek God and, in some way, the grace of God touches your life. Your victory may have come through a word or prayer or some other encouragement, but you absolutely know the Lord delivered you. Using the five smooth stones of divine grace, you defeated your Goliath.

But then, a few weeks or months later (or perhaps, years), suddenly all the old symptoms return with a vengeance. If you were struggling with an illness, it manifests now worse than ever;

if your battle was regarding a relationship, it seems like all progress has been lost and you are back to square one.

Have you ever been there? These negative experiences can drain the faith from your heart to such a degree that you feel you'll never recover the anticipation of faith again. A spiritual paralysis immobilizes your soul. You may still attend church, but your faith is unresponsive; when others testify of a healing or deliverance, you secretly wait, measuring the time until they, too, lose their healing.

For many, the result is one of severe disillusionment. The scripture says, "Hope deferred makes the heart sick" (Prov. 13:12). How can you trust God when it seems like He let you down? You wonder: Did I lose my breakthrough or was I only deceiving myself and never really had it?

But, dear one, it is very possible that what you are experiencing is an entirely new spiritual battle, not a loss of God's blessing. This new war is a very clever and effective deception that Satan uses to try and worm his way back into the lives of those delivered by God.

I had been praying about this very thing, this returning battle, when the Holy Spirit spoke to my heart, "Goliath had a brother." I was immediately reminded of David's war against the Philistine giant. We all know that David became a great hero by trusting God and defeating Goliath. However, later in his life other giants showed up to war against the Lord's servant. Amazingly, all of them were related to Goliath! Three of these giants were Goliath's actual children; one, was Goliath's brother (See 1 Chor. 20.). So, after defeating a giant once, David suddenly had to face another giant.

Get this point: Goliath had a brother that looked like him. We can imagine that the giant talked like Goliath, fought like him, and probably even smelled like him. Other than saying David was weary, the Bible is silent as to what might have been going through the king's mind. Perhaps he wondered, "I thought I killed you. What are you doing back?" But, Goliath hadn't come back. It was the giant's brother and children that returned; it just looked like the same battle! The truth was Goliath was dead.

Likewise, you also have had many successful victories. JUST BECAUSE THE CURRENT GIANT YOU ARE FACING LOOKS LIKE ONE YOU DEFEATED IN THE PAST, DON'T BUY THE LIE THAT YOU NEVER REALLY WON THE FIRST BATTLE!

By the strength of God's grace, you trusted the Almighty and conquered your Goliath. The first giant is dead. Satan is masquerading as your former enemy so he can slip past your faith and regain entrance into your life. Resist him. Stand in faith (Eph 6). Don't accept the lie that you were never delivered. The victory that overcomes the world is our faith (1 John 5:4). The Living God who helped you conquer Goliath will empower you to overcome his brother as well."

1 Peter 5:8-10 gives us a powerful instruction;

"Be sober, be vigilant; because your adversary the devil, as a roaring lion, walketh about, seeking whom he may devour:

Whom resist stedfast in the faith, knowing that the same afflictions are accomplished in your brethren that are in the world.

But the God of all grace, who hath called us unto his eternal glory by Christ Jesus, after that ye have suffered a while, make you perfect, stablish, strengthen, settle you."

Some of you are asking, "What are weapons of our Warfare? There are many ways to win a battle. There are also times when God gives us a specific strategy for a specific battle. There are 5 weapons you can always count on.

1st Weapon – Praise
2nd Weapon – Word of God
3rd Weapon – Blood of Jesus

4th Weapon – Prayer
5th Weapon – Power of Testimony

1st Weapon – Praise

Praise is a powerful weapon. I was preparing to speak one day when the Lord spoke to me and said, "use your weapon." I asked Him which one for this particular battle and He said "the weapon of praise". I have to tell you I was a little bewildered. I was in the heat of the battle and the last thing I felt like doing was praising God. But the Lord let me know that praise is a powerful weapon we seldom use. Praise is the smoke screen that confuses the enemy and ushers you into victory.

Praise is the last thing I feel like doing when I want to choke the adversary. But Paul and Silas found praise to be a powerful weapon while they were in the darkest part of their prison.

Acts 16:23, 25-26 tells us

> "And when they had laid many stripes upon them, they cast them into prison, charging the jailor to keep them safely:
>
> And at midnight Paul and Silas prayed, and sang praises unto God: and the prisoners heard them.
>
> And suddenly there was a great earthquake, so that the foundations of the prison were shaken:

and immediately all the doors were opened, and every one's bands were loosed."

God spoke a message to me one day. His message to me was "When praise becomes your greatest weapon." I learned that day through praise that many battles can be won. Is the answer always to praise in every battle? No. I know that the Bible commands us to praise Him at all times. But I am not talking about that. There are specific times in specific battles the Lord has certain strategies. It is when I don't feel like praising God that praise is my greatest weapon against the enemy. So the next time you get in the heat of the battle, throw on some praise and see what God will do.

Philippians 4:8 tells us "Finally, brethren, whatsoever things are true, whatsoever things are honest, whatsoever things are just, whatsoever things are pure, whatsoever things are lovely, whatsoever things are of good report; if there be any virtue, and if there be any praise, think on these things."

1 Peter 1:6-7 tells us, "Wherein ye greatly rejoice, though now for a season, if need be, ye are in heaviness through manifold temptations:

That the trial of your faith, being much more precious than of gold that perisheth, though it be tried with fire, might be found unto praise and honour and glory at the appearing of Jesus Christ:"

2nd Weapon – Word of God.

The Word of God is powerful! The Word of God is so powerful that it stands on its own. The Word was in the beginning and the Word will be in the end. The Word is God. When you exercise the Word in battle you are transporting God on the scene immediately.

When Jesus was in the wilderness being temped by satan, the devil tried to tempt Him by using the Word.

Luke 4:1-14

> "And Jesus being full of the Holy Ghost returned from Jordan, and was led by the Spirit into the wilderness,
>
> Being forty days tempted of the devil. And in those days he did eat nothing: and when they were ended, he afterward hungered.
>
> And the devil said unto him, If thou be the Son of God, command this stone that it be made bread.
>
> And Jesus answered him, saying, **It is written**, That man shall not live by bread alone, but by every **word of God**.
>
> And the devil, taking him up into an high mountain, shewed unto him all the kingdoms of the world in a moment of time.

And the devil said unto him, All this power will I give thee, and the glory of them: for that is delivered unto me; and to whomsoever I will I give it.

If thou therefore wilt worship me, all shall be thine.

And Jesus answered and said unto him, Get thee behind me, Satan: for **it is written**, Thou shalt worship the Lord thy God, and him only shalt thou serve.

And he brought him to Jerusalem, and set him on a pinnacle of the temple, and said unto him, If thou be the Son of God, cast thyself down from hence:

For **it is written**, He shall give his angels charge over thee, to keep thee:

And in their hands they shall bear thee up, lest at any time thou dash thy foot against a stone.

And Jesus answering said unto him, **It is said**, Thou shalt not tempt the Lord thy God.

And when the devil had ended all the temptation, he departed from him for a season.
And Jesus returned in the power of the Spirit into Galilee:...."

For every temptation, God used His Word against His adversary. The Word is powerful enough to set the enemy running. It is the one thing the enemy hates.

> Hebrews 4:12 say's "For the word of God is quick, and powerful, and sharper than any two-edged sword, piercing even to the dividing asunder of soul and spirit, and of the joints and marrow, and is a discerner of the thoughts and intents of the heart."

> Psalms 107:20 tells us "He sent his word, and healed them, and delivered them from their destructions."

The Word of God heals when we need healing.

> Psalms 119:105 says "Thy word is a lamp unto my feet, and a light unto my path."

The Word of God is a light to our feet when we need direction. So the Word of God is a powerful weapon that needs to be applied in every battle.

3rd Weapon – The Blood of Jesus

God has a plan for your life and you can fight this good fight of Faith. Stay strong in the Lord and know that as long as you are anointed you are going to fight. Understand there will always be spiritual warfare. This will never stop.

I use to catch myself looking for a "Utopia", thinking one day this spiritual warfare would all go away. It's never going to stop. The battle is never going to go away. We must lose the intimidation of the battle. We win every time.

What are we afraid of? I rebuke the fear. Stand up and be the warrior God has destined you to be.

Chapter Three

The Gifts of the Spirit

Paul begins his teaching of the Gifts of the Spirit by saying, "concerning Spiritual gifts, I would not have you ignorant."

One of the greatest hindrances to the Gifts of the Sprit has been this very thing; ignorance. There has been ignorance on both sides; the ones administering the Gifts and those being ministered to by the Gifts. In this chapter we will try to explain the Gifts of the Spirit and how they are to operate in the church. We understand that there are many Gifts in the Scripture. At this time we will discuss the traditional nine Gifts of the Spirit. Let us look at what they are and then discuss them individually.

1. Word of Wisdom
2. Word of Knowledge
3. Gift of Faith
4. Gifts of Healing
5. Working of Miracles
6. Prophecy
7. Discerning of Spirits
8. Tongues
9. Interpretation of Tongues

1 Corinthians 12:1-11

> Now concerning spiritual gifts, brethren, I would not have you ignorant.
>
> Ye know that ye were Gentiles, carried away unto these dumb idols, even as ye were led.
>
> Wherefore I give you to understand, that no man speaking by the Spirit of God calleth Jesus accursed: and that no man can say that Jesus is the Lord, but by the Holy Ghost.
>
> Now there are diversities of gifts, but the same Spirit.
>
> And there are differences of administrations, but the same Lord.
>
> And there are diversities of operations, but it is the same God which worketh all in all.

But the manifestation of the Spirit is given to every man to profit withal.

For to one is given by the Spirit the word of wisdom; to another the word of knowledge by the same Spirit;

To another faith by the same Spirit; to another the gifts of healing by the same Spirit;

To another the working of miracles; to another prophecy; to another discerning of spirits; to another divers kinds of tongues; to another the interpretation of tongues:

But all these worketh that one and the selfsame Spirit, dividing to every man severally as he will.

Verse 11 tells us that all of these work through the Spirit of God in a believer's life, and that a believer may have several Gifts at one time.

The Word of Wisdom & Knowledge

The Word of Wisdom to me is the most important Gift of the Spirit. Without the Word of Wisdom, all the other Gifts of the Spirit can be misused. James 1:5 tells us, "If any of you lack Wisdom, let Him ask of God, that giveth to all men liberally, and upbraideth not, and it shall be given him." The Gifts of the Spirit are powerful tools in a believer's life. These tools must be used with the Wisdom of God or they can become destructive. The Word of Wisdom is a supernatural Wisdom that comes from the Spirit of God. This Wisdom will direct you in how to best administer the other Gifts of the Spirit. The Word of Wisdom works very closely with the Word of Knowledge.

The Word of Knowledge is simply supernatural knowledge about things you had no way of knowing. God uses the Word of Knowledge Gifts to build Faith and to edify the body of Christ. If the knowledge you receive about an individual does not build their Faith or their walk with God, it should not be administered to them. It is important to understand that the Gifts are to edify the body. Ephesians 4:12 tells us "that the work of the ministry is to edify the body of Christ." To edify here means to build up. This is where the Word of Wisdom comes to direct the Knowledge that has been received. God may reveal that a person has cancer (knowledge), but this person may not be aware of this cancer, so for us to say "You have cancer" may cause this person to be afraid. The Word of Wisdom would direct the Word of Knowledge to be more general. Instead of calling out the specifics (cancer) it would better benefit the person by saying "there is a physical need in your body that God would like to heal." Every individual is different and will handle the Word of Knowledge differently. This is why the Word of Wisdom is so important.

Another example of how the Word of Wisdom works with the Word of Knowledge is, God speaks to you that this person has been wounded deep in their spirit. Now you must ask God for the Wisdom to minister to this person. Since they are already wounded, they must be handled properly. The Word of Wisdom may give you the okey to minister to this person openly or you may be prompted to minister to this person one on one as not to embarrass them. The Holy Ghost is a gentleman and will not embarrass anyone He is trying to help. Always keep in mind we are trying to build people up not tear them down. Every situation is different, so God will direct you in how to handle every individual.

There was a Pastor's wife who came to our meeting one night. She pulled her back out while working at her house that day. She could not stand straight up but was hunched over and in a lot of pain. She came believing God would heal her. When she came in I did not need a Word of Knowledge. It was obvious she needed healing. She came to the front to be prayed for and the Holy Ghost spoke to me a Word of Wisdom on how she would get her healing. What was strange to me was, it did not sound like Wisdom. I was prompted to drop my ink pen on the floor and tell her to pick it up. Natural wisdom said this is crazy, she is in pain. She can barely move and you are going to ask her to bend over and pick up an ink pen. However, I knew the voice of the Lord, so I dropped my pen on the floor and said with boldness "pick up my pen". She bent over in tremendous pain and grabbed my pen. When she touched the pen, the pain left and she began shouting and dancing around the front of the building. Praise God!! I knew what she needed, but I needed the Wisdom to help her receive healing. Pray that God will give you more Wisdom and do not rely on the wisdom of this world, but upon the Wisdom of God.

The Word of Knowledge is a unique gift that God uses to build Faith. When people realize that you know nothing about their life and all of a sudden God opens up the book of their life, it tells them God knows more about them than they thought. The Word of Knowledge is never to bring glory to the person being used, but to bring glory to God. The Word of Knowledge tells people that God cares about them and their situation. It tells them that God has heard their prayers and He has not forgotten them.

The Word of Wisdom and the Word of Knowledge are Gifts that are needed much in the church. If you have not been used by God in these Gifts, pray that God will develop them in your life. If God is using you already in this area, then pray that the voice of the Lord becomes clearer than ever before. Let God use you for His glory.

Gift of Faith

The Gift of Faith is my favorite of all the Gifts. The Gift of Faith is a supernatural impartation of Faith. When someone is being used in the Gift of Faith those around receive the Faith to believe God for the impossible. You can see Faith begin to rise in the believer's hearts when the Word of God is being preached. This is because they are preaching the Word of Faith. This is very powerful in itself, but when someone preaches the Word of God with the Gift of Faith it becomes dynamic. I have witnessed the Faith of God move through a service and people were healed and delivered with no one laying hands on them. The Gift of Faith was imparted to them and they received their miracle.

We were preaching in Louisiana one night, and while I was preaching the Gift of Faith began to operate. A man came to the front of the building and said, "I don't need this insulin anymore. God just healed me of Sugar Diabetes." Praise God!

In another service a woman asked to testify before we closed the service. She said she had been having trouble in her arm and shoulder, but as we preached the Word and told about God healing others she said, "God is no respecter of persons. If God healed them He will heal me." She raised her hand during the preaching and God healed her arms and shoulders. How did it happen? The Gift of Faith was released and she believed the Word of God and was healed.

Acts 14:7-10, Paul was preaching the Gospel and a man lame from his mothers womb received the Faith to be healed. Paul perceived this and said to the man "stand up". The scripture goes on to say that "he leaped up and walked."

The Gift of Faith does not just happen when someone is preaching. The Gift of Faith can work anywhere, anytime. There were times when we were talking with people and you could feel the Gift of Faith enter their hearts. This is when you need to speak the Word with boldness. If it is healing they need, then speak healing. If it is deliverance they need, then speak it. Many times when talking to someone about the Holy Ghost, you can feel their Faith begin to rise. It is then that they are ready to receive the Holy Ghost. They don't need an alter call or their favorite song played. They are ready to receive.

Have you ever been in service when the Word was being preached and people began to receive the Holy Ghost? This is the Gift of Faith in operation. When you sense the Gift of faith in a service, it is important to flow with the moving of the Spirit.

The Gift of Faith can also operate in giving. There are times when the Gift of Faith will move upon people to give sacrificially. Many times it will be in a way they would not ordinarily give. They will give because they know God is going to bless them. One night I felt very strong to challenge the people to give. I didn't tell any stories. I did not make the people feel guilty. I simply allowed the Gift of Faith to work through me. People began to bring their offerings to the Lord. In about ten minutes, $15,000 was laying on the altar. As people began to give, they also began to be healed and receive the Holy Ghost. It was awesome to watch the Gift of Faith move through the whole congregation.

In the hour that we live in, we desperately need the Gift of Faith in our lives. The world has no hope. They are coming to the church broken and bruised. They have lost their Faith to believe, but we as mighty men and women of God can impart to them the gift of Faith. They will believe and be set free.

A great hindrance to walking in the Gift of Faith is education. I am not against education, seeing I have a Master's degree in Theo-centric counseling and a Doctorate degree in Religious Education. What I am against is allowing education to replace Faith and walking in the Spiritual.

If we are not careful, much learning can lead us to madness and away from leaning on the voice of the Lord. It seems as time progresses and knowledge increases that people of this age rely on psychological and analytical thinking instead of the ways of the Spirit. Worldly knowledge amounts to little if our lives are not based upon blind Faith.

Yes, I believe in balance and I believe that we live in a natural world. However, I also feel we have to be careful how much the world indoctrinates their worldly views into our minds. If we are not careful this can over-ride our Spiritual life; resulting in a lack of Spiritual manifestations such as miracles, signs and wonders.

In Dr. Cho's book "The Fourth Dimension" he writes about a powerful subject in the 2nd chapter entitled, "The Fourth Dimension". This here is what I believe is one of the missing ingredients to seeing the miraculous.

"As there are certain steps that we must follow in order for our Faith to be properly incubated, there is also a central truth concerning the nature of Faith's realm that we need to understand. The most important lessons that I have learned about the nature of the realm of Faith began as a result of what was at first an unpleasant experience.

In America ministers do not have this kind of problem, but in the Orient I have real trouble in preaching about the miraculous power of God, for in Buddhism monks also have performed fantastic miracles. Just recently in Korea one woman was dying from a case of terminal cancer, and no doctor could cure her. She went to many churches, then to a Buddhist monk. He took her to a grotto where there were many praying, and she was completely healed and cleansed, and the cancer disappeared.

In Korea, many people involved in yoga are healing the sick by yoga meditation. When attending meetings of the Japanese Sokagakkai, many are healed, some of stomach ulcers, the deaf and dumb hearing and speaking, and the blind seeing. So naturally we Christians, especially Pentecostal Christians, have real difficulty in explaining these occurrences. You cannot put these things away simply as a manifestation of the devil. But if the devil could do these things, why should not the Church of Jesus Christ do all the more?

I was quite troubled one day for many of our Christians were not considering God's miracles to be of importance. They said, "Oh, how can we believe in God as an absolute Divine Being? How can we call the Jehovah God the unique creator in heavenly places? We see miracles in Buddhism, miracles in yoga, and miracles in the Oriental Sokagakkai. We see many miracles in the Oriental religions. Why should we claim Jehovah God as the only creator of the universe?

But I knew that our God was the unique God, the only God, and the creator of the universe. So I made their questions a matter of prayer before God. I fasted and prayed, seeking the faith of the Lord, and His answers. Then a glorious revelation came to my heart, and I received a clear explanation. And from that time on I began to explain these things through my lectures in my church in Korea. Now I can give a satisfying reply to any of those questions, and I can easily give explanations, explanations as clear as a sunny day. Let me explain it to you.

In the universe there are three types of Spirits – the Holy Spirit of God, the spirit of the devil, and the human spirit. When you study geometry you put up two points, one here, and one there, and if you draw a line between the two you call it one dimension. It is just one line between the points, one dimension. But if you add line upon line by the hundreds of thousands, then one dimension naturally creates a second dimension, a plane. And if you stack up planes one upon another then it becomes cubic; this is called the third dimension. The material world and the whole earth belong to the third dimension.

This first dimension, a line, is contained in, and therefore controlled by, the second dimension, a plane; the second dimension is included in, and therefore controlled by, the third dimension, the cube. Who then creates, contains, and controls the third dimension, the cubical world? You have the answer when you open the Bible and read in Genesis 1:2: "And the earth was without form, and void; and darkness was upon the face of the deep. And the Spirit of God moved upon the face of the waters."

But if you look into the original language of that scripture, it carries the meaning that the Spirit of the Lord was incubating over the waters, brooding over the waters. This chaotic world belonged to the third dimension, but the Holy Spirit, who is pictured here incubating on the third dimension, belongs to the Fourth dimension. So the Spiritual kingdom of Faith belongs to the Fourth dimension.

Since the Spiritual world hugged the third dimension, incubating on the third dimension, it was by this incubation of the fourth dimension of the third dimension that the earth was recreated. A new order was given out of the old, and life was given from death; beauty from ugliness; cleanliness from those things dirty; and abundance from poverty. Everything was created beautiful and wonderful by the incubation of the fourth dimension.

Then God spoke to my heart, "Son, as the second dimension includes and controls the first dimension, and the third dimension includes and controls the second dimension, so the fourth dimension includes and controls the third dimension, producing a creation of order and beauty. The Spirit is the fourth dimension. Every human being is a spiritual being as well as a physical being. They have the fourth dimension as well as the third dimension in their hearts." So men, by exploring their spiritual sphere of the fourth dimension through the development of concentrated visions and dreams in their imaginations, can brood over and incubate the third dimension, influencing and changing it. This is what the Holy Spirit taught me.

So naturally these yoga people and Buddhist believers could explore and develop their human fourth dimension, their spiritual sphere; with clear-cut visions and mental pictures of health they could incubate over their bodies. By natural order the fourth dimension has power over the third dimension, and the human spirit, within limitations, has the power to give order and creation. God gave power to human beings to control the material world and to have dominion over material things, a responsibility they can carry out through the fourth dimension. Now unbelievers, by exploring and developing their inner spiritual being in such a way, can carry out dominion upon their third dimension, which includes their physical sickness and diseases.

The Holy Spirit said to me, "Look at the Sokagakkai. They belong to satan; the human spirit joins up with the spirit of the evil fourth dimension, and with the evil fourth dimension they carry out dominion over their bodies and circumstances." The Holy Spirit showed me that it was in this manner that the magicians in Egypt carried out dominion over various occurrences, just as Moses did.

God then taught me that since we can link our Spirit's fourth dimension to the fourth dimension of the Holy Spirit, we can have all the more dominion over circumstances. Praise God! We can become fantastically creative, and we can exercise great control and power over the third dimension.

After receiving this revelation from the Lord I began to easily explain the happenings and miracles of other religions. People would come and challenge me, "We can do the same miracles."

I would say, "Yes, I know you can. It's because you have the fourth dimension in your spirit. You are developing your spirit and carrying out dominion over your body and circumstances. But that spirit is not a spirit with salvation, even though you can exercise those kinds of miracles.

"You are linked to the evil fourth dimension. The fourth dimension has power to carry out dominion over the third dimension. You do have certain limited powers to carry out dominion over the third dimension, influencing your circumstances."

The Role of the Subconscious

In America I saw a lot of mind-expanding books, and I see similar things happening everywhere because of all this emphasis on the subconscious. What is the subconscious? The subconscious is your spirit. The Bible calls the subconscious the inner man, the man hidden in your heart.

Before psychology found the subconscious, Apostle Paul had already discovered it 2,000 years before, writing of the inner, hidden man. The Bible had that truth 2,000 years ago. Now scientist and psychologist make a great affair of this discovery, digging into the ideas of the subconscious and trying to direct its energies. Though the subconscious is in the fourth dimension, therefore having certain limited power, however, a great amount of deception is involved in what these people claim.

I was amazed coming to America and reading the books some American ministers gave me, for these books had almost made the subconscious into an almighty god, and that is a great deception. The subconscious has certain influence, but it is quite limited, and cannot create like our Almighty God can. I have begun to see in America the Unitarian Church try to develop the subconscious, the fourth dimension of the human spirit, and put that human spirit in the place of Jesus Christ; this indeed is great deception and a great danger.

While we do recognize certain realities and truths in these teachings, it is also important to realize that the devil occupies an evil fourth dimension. God, however, is holy, unique, and Almighty. The fourth dimension is always creating and giving order, and carrying out dominion over the third dimensions by the means of incubation. In Genesis, the Spirit of the Lord was incubating, brooding over the water; He was like a hen sitting on her eggs, incubating them and hatching chickens. In much the same manner the Holy Spirit incubates the third dimension, so does the evil spirit incubate.

I was watching the television news in the U.S., and there was a great controversy in one area because a man was murdered, the lawyer claiming that this young murderer was intoxicated by violent television programs. There was a certain truth in that, for this boy, after watching television, began to exercise his fourth dimension. He was incubating on those acts of violence, and naturally he hatched the same sin.

The Language of the Fourth Dimension

My ministry has been revolutionized by discovering the truth of the fourth dimension, and you can revolutionize your life with it. You may wonder how we can incubate our subconscious. We dwell in limited bodies. Whereas the Holy Spirit in His omnipresence can simply incubate over the whole earth. We are so limited in space and time, and the only way for us to incubate is through our imaginations, through our visions and our dreams.

This is the reason the Holy Spirit comes to cooperate with us-to create, by helping young men to see visions, and old men to dream dreams, through envisioning and dreaming dreams we can kick away the wall of limitations, and can stretch out the universe. That is the reason that God's Word says, "Where there is no vision the people perish." If you have no vision, you are not being creative; and if you stop being creative, then you are going to perish.

Visions and dreams are the language of the fourth dimension, and the Holy Spirit communicates through them. Only through a vision and a dream can you visualize and dream bigger churches. You can visualize a new mission field; you can visualize the increase of your church. Through visualizing and dreaming you can incubate your future and hatch the results. Let me substantiate this with scriptural examples.

Do you know why Adam and Eve fell from grace? The devil knew that the fourth dimension visions and dreams in a person's mind could create a definite result. The devil used a tactic based on this premise; he invited Eve saying, "Eve, come over and look at that fruit on the forbidden tree. Looking at it is harmless, so why don't you come over and just look at it?

So since simply looking at the fruit seemed to be harmless, Eve went and looked at the fruit of the tree. She looked at that tree not only once, but she kept looking. The Bible says in Genesis, the third chapter, verse six, "And when the woman saw that the tree was good for food...she took of the fruit thereof, and did eat." Before she partook she saw the tree, also seeing this fruit in her imagination. She played with the idea of eating the fruit, and brought that to her fourth dimension.

In the fourth dimension either good or evil is created. Eve brought that picture of the tree and fruit deep into her imagination, seeing the fruit clearly, imagining that it could make her as wise as God. Then she felt so attracted to that tree, it was as if she were being pulled toward it; next she took the fruit of the tree and ate, then gave some to her husband. And with that action, she fell.

If seeing is not important, why did the angel of God give such a grievous judgement to the wife of Lot? In Genesis 19:17 the Bible reads, "Escaped for they life; look not behind thee." It is a simple command: do not look behind you. However, when you read Genesis 19:26, you discover that Lot's wife looked back and became a pillar of salt. She received that grievous judgement just because she looked back.

God has been using this language of the Holy Spirit to change many lives. Look carefully when you read Genesis 13:14-15, "And the Lord said unto Abraham, after that Lot was separated from him,

'Lift up now thine eyes, and look from the place where thou art, northward, southward, and eastward, and westward: For all the land which thou seest, to thee will I give it, and to thy seed forever.'"

God did not say, "Oh, Abraham, I'll give you Cannan. Just claim it." No, very specifically, God told him to stand from his place, look northward, southward, eastward, and westward, and that He would give that land to Abraham and his descendants.

I wish he could have had a helicopter, for then he could have gone up high and seen all the Middle East, and thus avoided the many past and present problems there. But since he had no binoculars and no helicopter, his vision was limited.

Seeing is possession. Abraham saw the land; he then went back to his tent, and to his bed, to dream of the land which were going to become his. In his fourth dimension the Holy spirit began to use that language. The Holy Spirit began to carry out dominion.

It is interesting that Abraham got his child Isaac when he was one hundred years old, and when Sarah was ninety. When Abraham was almost one hundred years old, and Sarah almost ninety, God came and told him that he was going to have a child. When God came to him and said, "You are going to have a son," Abraham laughed and laughed. This means that Abraham was totally unbelieving.

We also see that Sarah laughed behind the tent. God asked, "Sarah, why are you laughing?" she replied, "No, I didn't laugh." But God said, "No, you laughed."

Both Abraham and Sarah laughed. They were both unbelieving. But God had a way to make them believe, for God used the fourth dimension, the language of the Holy Spirit. One night God said to Abraham, "Come out." In the Middle East the humidity is very low, so in the night you can see the many stars sparkling. Abraham came out, and God said, "Abraham, count the number of the stars." So he started counting the stars.

Scientists say that with the human eye we can count 6,000 stars. So we can imagine Abraham kept on counting and counting, eventually forgetting the number. He finally said, "Father, I can't count them all." Then the Father said, "Your children are going to become as numerous as those stars."

I imagine that Abraham was struck with emotion. Soon tears began to well up in his eyes, and his vision became completely blurred. When he looked up at the stars, all he could see were the faces of his children, and suddenly he felt that he was hearing them call to him, "Father Abraham!" he was all shaken up, and when he returned to his tent he was shaking all over. He could not sleep when he closed his eyes, for he saw all the stars changing into the faces of his descendants, and once again shouting, "Father Abraham!"

Those pictures came to his mind again and again, and became his own dreams and pictures. Those pictures immediately became part of his fourth dimension, in the language of spiritual visions and dreams. These visions and dreams carried dominion over his one-hundred-year-old body, and it was soon transformed as if it were like a young body from that time on he believed the Word of God, and he praised the Lord.

Who could change Abraham so much? The Holy Spirit, because God had applied the law of the fourth dimension, the language of the Holy Spirit. A vision and dream changed Abraham, not only his mind, but his physical body as well. Not only he, but his wife, too, were wonderfully rejuvenated. Later on in the Bible you can read how King Abimelech tried to make Sarah his concubine: ninety-year-old Sarah, who had been rejuvenated through the law and language of the fourth dimension.

We are not common animals. When God created us He created in us the fourth dimension, the spiritual world. Then God said, "You carry out dominion over all the third dimension."

I cannot carry out my ministry of winning souls by simply knocking on doors, struggling and working myself to death. I use the way of faith, and the church is growing by leaps and bounds. And even though our church has more than 50,000 registered members, when I go to the office I do not have a great deal to do, for I follow a path of faith, and am not constantly striving in my flesh to bring to pass those things that the Holy Spirit can easily do.

I learned that even while I minister in foreign countries I can go into the fourth dimension of the Holy spirit, and I tell Him what is needed in my church in Korea, and He carries out the work. I call my wife about every two days, and she is continually giving me information which has served sometimes as a blow to my ego. I used to think that the members of my church would be very anxious for my return from my trips abroad; they would all be waiting for me, and I was sure that Sunday service attendance would go down. She would say, "Don't brag about it. The church is doing all the better, even without having you."[i]

I found that what Dr. Cho was teaching here was what we call "Faith". Hebrews 11:1 tells us, "Now faith is the substance of things **hoped for**, the **evidence** of things **not seen**." Faith is simply this, speaking, seeing, and walking in what is not there yet. By Faith we act as if those things we are wanting to experience are already manifest.

Too many times we walk in reality instead of walking in the Faith that God has given us. I remember one time Rev. T.W. Barnes telling my husband and I if we wanted to see more miracles and healings, we had to start seeing them happen in the Spirit. I believe what He was really saying is, you have to allow your Faith to produce the evidence so you may have the very things you are asking God for. If you can't see it, you will inevitably struggle to receive the promises God has for you. You must be able to lay aside what reality is telling you and step into the realm of the Spirit to grasp the thing that hasn't manifested itself yet.

All answers start in the spirit. It is only a matter of time before they make it to the flesh. The main thing is for us to hold on to our Faith and wait until that thing hoped for is made evident in our circumstances. Too many times we become frustrated when the manifestation does not appear right away, but we must hold fast to what we know is the Spirit instead of what we see with our fleshly eyes. I often am tempted to go by what I see instead of what I know, and this is a great hindrance in seeing the supernatural miracles of God created. We must be able to overcome what these fleshly eyes see and see with the eyes of Faith.

The place we must enter into is "blind Faith"; Faith that proclaims before we can actually see the result. Romans 4:17 tells us, "(As it is written, I have made thee a father of many nations,) before him whom he believed, even God, who quickeneth the dead, and **calleth those things which be not as though they were.**" The impossible is attained when we grasp a hold of this "blind Faith."

Gifts of Healing

One of the first things that stand out to me is the scripture reveals this Gift is plural. It states "Gifts of Healing." Healing can take place in many different areas. There can be healing for the body, mind, spirit, family, church…..etc.

Secondly, healing does not take place overnight. It is a process of time. We always want an immediate miracle but God sometimes chooses the process of healing. We need to understand that it does not matter how we receive our deliverance as long as we receive it. We have prayed for people that had sugar diabetes and they said they knew God had touched them, yet it took several days for the sugar to come back to normal. This is the Gift of Healing in operation. The Gifts of Healing can also be seen when ministering with an individual that has been verbally abused. Many times God will help this person heal over time. Healing will come to the mind and the spirit. We have witnessed individuals make a total turn-round once the healing process was completed. The believer must not be discouraged when they do not receive a miracle; that is an immediate deliverance, but must understand that God uses not only miracles but the process of healing. Lacking this understanding has caused many people to miss their deliverance. When you are prayed for, remember that God will perform deliverance through the Gifts of Healing or the working of Miracles.

Working of Miracles

A miracle is a supernatural, instant deliverance. The working of miracles is an exciting Gift to be a part of. The working of Miracles happens immediately. We have witnessed people full of fear come for deliverance and have seen them instantly set free. That is the working of Miracles.

We were in the state of Ohio preaching a revival and God began to perform mighty Miracles physically. In the service there were three or four people that had bone spurs in the heel of their feet. They came to the prayer line and God instantly removed the bone spurs and they were healed. One lady we never even prayed for, but while we were praying for a man with a bone spur, she said, "When God healed that man ahead of me, God also healed me." Her bone spurs were completely gone. God was using the working of miracles and the Gift of Faith at the same time. Another lady in that same revival had one leg that was several inches shorter than the other. We laid hands on her and watched God straighten the leg the same as the other. The foot on that leg had been deformed from birth. It was turned to the inside of the leg with her toes completely drawn under the foot. In an instance God lengthened the leg and strengthened the foot and healed the deformity. It was a notable miracle. God taught me the difference between miracles and healing that night. The next night she came back and told us that her toes on her healed leg had been curled up under her foot for years and was still like that when she got home. However, the next morning when she awoke she felt something different. When she rolled the covers back she told her husband to look at her toes. They were straight and normal. Praise God!! Why did God wait until the next morning to do this? He was letting us understand the differences between Healing and the working of Miracles.

Remember, it does not matter how you receive your deliverance as long as you receive it.

The closer we get to the coming of the Lord, the more frequent the working of miracles will become. God will use notable miracles to get the attention of people. All throughout the book of Acts you find God uses the working of Miracles to start great revivals. In the last several years we have seen notable miracles begin to increase. God is not finished. He is going to do even greater miracles in the days to come. Pray for God to use you in the working of Miracles. It only takes one miracle to bring revival to a city.

Gift of Prophecy

The Gift of Prophecy is the ability to for-tell future events. Prophecy is a great tool that God uses to build Faith in people. For example, John is not sure of Gods existence, or his faith is weak at this time in his life. God one night uses the Gift of Prophecy to minister to John about some specific things that are about to happen. Over the next few weeks these signs began to take place just as God had spoken. Now John knows by experience the power and love of God.

The Gift of Prophecy can also be used to bring peace and comfort. God has used us many times to Prophecy that the storm is almost over. God has heard your prayer and knows you can't take much more. God is about to speak "peace be still". I have watched people's countenance began to change as the peace of God came running in like a river.

The Word of Prophecy is a sure word to hold on to. I have waited as long as five years for some prophecies God spoke to me. God's Word will always come to pass. You must hold on to the Word of Prophecy with steadfast Faith. No matter what comes or goes I believe what God said. You may receive a negative report. Do not let it affect your Faith. What did God say? Are you going to take their word or Gods Word? Who shall believe the report of the Lord? You and I shall believe the report of the Lord. We know that Gods Word is a sure foundation. His Word shall come to pass. God can turn your situation around in one night. Joseph, don't worry because you have a promise. God took Joseph from the prison to the palace over night. God can fulfill His Word so fast it will blow your mind. What a mighty God we serve.

I remember one night praying for a couple and prophesying to them that God was about to give them the desires of their heart. I did not know their desire was to have a baby. She had some physical problems and had not been able to conceive. When she would conceive her body would reject the seed and miscarry. After the prophecy they were rejoicing and praising God. They were excited about what God said. Two nights later she came to church and it was obvious that her Faith had taken a hard blow. She had no joy. She was weeping. She was having a difficult time worshiping. God spoke to me and said, "Tell her I have not forgotten what I spoke to her. It does not matter what her body is telling her. I am going to do what I said. Just believe what God has said."

When I ministered to her, her Faith was restored and she began praising God. Her tears of sorrow were turned into tears of Joy. I did not know it, but that day at work she began to have great pain. She had felt that pain before and it signified that her body was trying to reject producing this baby. She said she cried to God and told Him that she believed His Word. When she got to church all she needed was a confirmation that everything would be all right. Everything turned out fine and in nine months they had a healthy baby boy. God keeps His promises. Keep your eyes on the promise of God. When God says it, it will happen. Hang in there. It is going to happen.

Discerning of Spirits

The Gift of Discerning of Spirits is very vital for the church. To discern the Spirit is the ability to tell truth from error. I have heard people say the right things but not in the right spirit. It is not enough to speak what sounds right. There must be a right Spirit for it to be truth. I John 4:1 say's, "Beloved, believe not every spirit, but try the spirits whether they are of God: because many false prophets are gone out into the world." Strong's Greek Lexicon tells us the word TRY means "to TEST (literally or figuratively) by implication, to approve." Thayer Greek Lexicon say's TRY means to "EXAMINE, TO SCRUTINIZE (to see whether a thing is genuine or not)." The reason we must test the Spirit is because there are false Prophets in the world. Jesus said in Mathew 24:11, "And many false prophets shall rise, and shall deceive many." In verse 24 He say's, not only will there be false prophets, but also false Christ's.... "and shall show great signs and wonders, in so much that, if it were possible, they would deceive the very elect." The Gift of Discerning of Spirits will prevent this deception. We talk a lot about false prophets but the discerning of Spirits is for more than just false prophets. Paul talks about False brethren (see 2 Corinthians 11:26,

Galatians 2:4) who were brought in unaware. Paul say's that these false brethren will try to bring us into bondage.

When I was just starting in ministry there was a man that came into our fellowship. By looking at the outward appearance you would say everything looked okey. He preached the Truth. He and His family had a good outward standard of Holiness. He seemed to have plenty of money. God must be blessing Him. But for some reason, I did not feel comfortable around him. I have learned since then this uncomfortable feeling should not be ignored. This man slowly began to pull in a following. (I want to state here that most of these men were good men that I still respect to this day. I want them to know that I mean no disrespect in sharing this story). This man began to offer big returns on investments. By looking at what he drove, where he lived, and how he entertained, he must know what he was doing. However, this man ended up being a crook. He embezzled the money and left good brethren hung out to dry. Many have suffered great losses financially. Being able to discern false brethren would have prevented this from happening. We must be careful and make sure we are not being led by our emotions or our feelings. You cannot trust your emotions or feelings when it comes to discerning the Spirit. We must test the Spirit to see if God is in it.

Peter also tells us to be aware of false teachers (see II Peter 2:1). Peter said they would bring in damnable heresies. A false teacher is someone who takes the Word of Truth and twists it into false doctrine. We must discern the Spirit of these people. They can be so cunning with the Word and unless you are led by the Spirit, you will be deceived. We must always ask what is right behind these teachings. Where will it lead us to? Will we be more like Jesus? By asking honest questions like these we can discern the Spirits to see if they be of God.

Gift Of Tongues & Gift of Interpretation of Tongues

The Gift of Tongues and the Interpretation of Tongues are two of the most common Gifts. From my experience, these two Gifts are used more than the other nine gifts. The majority of us have witnessed and been blessed by these two Gifts on different occasions. The Gift of Tongues can operate separately from the Gift of Interpretation of Tongues. Many use the Gift of Tongues in prayer by praying in the Spirit. Paul said when one speaks in tongues they edify themselves (see I Corinthians 13:4). When someone interprets tongues, the whole body can be edified. I have witnessed these two Gifts, not only for edification, but also for rebuke and judgment. They are also used to bring repentance. The Gift of Tongues and Interpretation can be a powerful tool when used properly. If not, they bring confusion. Let me say here that it is not the Gift that causes confusion, but the improper use of the Gifts.

I have been in churches where these Gifts were used as leverage to promote personal agenda's. This is not of God but flesh. I would not want to be in anyone's shoes who purposely and willfully misused the Gifts of God. To say God is speaking when God is not speaking is nothing more than a lie. I think we must use extreme caution when it comes to "thus saith the Lord".

You may ask, "How do I know if it is God or not?" Number one, it should always agree with God's Word. Secondly, it should be done in a right Spirit. If you see these Gifts operating outside the Word of God, causing confusion or hurt, you should be cautious to the real spirit that is behind the individual involved.

I was in a service one night where three ladies felt that they were hearing from God more than the Pastor. One would begin speaking in tongues and another would interpret that the Pastor needed to do this or that. It was obvious that these women had not heard from God, but were walking in their own carnal nature.

Timing is also very important. I have noticed that when God is ready to use the Gift of Tongues and Interpretation there will always be a "Holy Hush" that comes upon the congregation. Even the babies will become quiet. There will be a strong presence of God that begins to hover over the congregation. You can sense God is about to do something great. If you have the Gift of Tongues and feel Him moving in that direction, pray for Wisdom that God open a clear door for you to walk in.

I Corinthians 14:13 say's, "Wherefore let him that speaketh in an unknown tongue pray that he may interpret". What Paul is saying is, if you speak forth in an unknown tongue and there is no interpreter present, you then need to ask God to give you the interpretation so the whole body will be edified. Paul went on to say in verse 27 thru 28, "If any man speak in an unknown tongue, let it be by two, or at the most by three, and that by course; and let one interpret. But if there be no interpreter, let him keep silence in the church; and let him speak to himself, and to God."

Paul is letting us know we don't need ten people speaking in the Gift of Tongues for God to get the message across. He said at the most, three, and they need to be done by course or one at a time. Paul then teaches us if we know we do not have the Gift of Interpretation of Tongues and no other interpreter is present, then we should "keep silence" in the church. The reason for this is so we do not cause confusion. I Corinthians 14:33 is clear that "God is not the author of confusion, but of peace, as in all churches of the saints."

We must keep in mind that all the Gifts of the Spirit are to edify (that is to build up) the body of Christ. Let us not be ignorant concerning Spiritual Gifts. For God has placed the Gifts of the Spirit in the church to bring Glory to His name.

Chapter Four

Fear of Failure

Fear is a powerful thing. I have learned that fear presents itself in many different forms. In this chapter I want to talk to you about the "fear of failure". Failure, while doing your best, is a blow to the best of us, especially when we have done our best to succeed or be right and still meet defeat. That kind of disappointment can be devastating.

I will never forget the first time I began to be used by God. First off, let me explain that I didn't know I was being used by God. I knew I had these thoughts and feelings, but didn't know they were the Lord trying to teach me how to walk in the Holy Ghost.

As I grew up in the church, I had the privilege to sit under prophetic ministry in my church. Bishop L.A. Parent was without doubt a Prophet in his own time. He was a man that could look you in the eye and see all the way to the sole of your feet. He was simply hooked up with a divine flow. So being blessed to have this heritage, I never understood that as I sat on the front row as a child I was receiving this prophetic seed into my life as I continued to grow. As Bishop L.A. died, it seemed like the prophetic ministry seemed to fade away. Little did I know that God had placed a tremendous anointing in my life with great prophetic tendencies. Because I was not mentored by prophetic people in my younger years I just viewed me as being different.

As I started to grow, I understood that I began to know things that I shouldn't have known otherwise. God would speak to me about things that were going on in people's lives. In my youthfulness, I thought that everyone would want to know these same things. So I proceeded to tell those in authority what I was feeling and was quickly set in my place. I am sure these things were done with good intentions, but they undermined that still small voice that was trying to teach me how to hear the Lord. I began to understand that being used by God entailed much pain and separation. Why weren't there more people like me? Was I strange? Was something wrong with me? If God always translated us out of these learning experiences, we would forfeit the greatest lessons life has a way of teaching.

As I was walking and messing up, the enemy made sure my failures were magnified. In doing this, there was a great feeling of intimidation and insecurity when it came to walking in that "still small voice". Every time I seemed to exercise my gift, I always got shot to the ground.

Let me stop and say here, if you are going to be used by God, the enemy is going to make sure that every stumble you make is intensified so he can convince you that you are a failure and you need to take another direction. But I have to say that all those painful experiences I went through developed in me great character and strength. It also taught me that I can do nothing without the Lord. Another thing it taught me was, even with Him there would be times I would fall like Peter did. The key was to get back up and not let the lie of the enemy deceive me into thinking I wasn't called or anointed.

You see, the enemy wants your failures to produce such a fear that you won't want to try and succeed again. If the enemy can get your failures to overshadow your accomplishments he can get you to withdraw and forfeit the anointing that is on your life.

Failures are a part of maturing and growing in God. Failures teach us many things. They teach me how to never put faith in my own abilities. They teach me how to fall and get up again. They also teach me how to grow in grace. Without failures in our lives, we would never appreciate our accomplishments. There is something about failure that makes our successes taste sweeter.

Failure is a familiar experience for all of us. As Christians, we are especially aware of that sinking feeling we get when we know that we have disappointed God. The apostle Peter knew failure intimately. Several New Testament accounts chronicle the details of his many failures. Yet, repeatedly, Christ forgave Peter, restored him and granted him renewed hope.

It is interesting to examine the manner in which Jesus restored Peter. The Lord's first words to Peter were, "Come follow Me." Likewise, His last words to Peter were, "You must follow Me." During every step of the journey between those two challenges, Peter never stopped following, but he often stumbled.

At the very moment that Peter submitted his life to Jesus Christ, this plain fisherman became a new person with new priorities. He did not, however, become a *perfect* person, and he never ceased being himself.

We may wonder what qualities Jesus saw in this impulsive man, Peter, that He would choose him as one of the twelve apostles. But it is important to understand that when God chooses followers, He does not see us as we *are*, but as what we can *become*, as He faithfully transforms us into His image. God is looking for *real* people who can be changed by His love. He then uses them as ambassadors of grace, to carry His message of love to others. He seeks followers who, because of the changes in their lives, no longer glorify themselves, but glorify the Lord Jesus.

Knowing that Jesus accepted Peter in spite of his failures, and used him to accomplish mighty works, gives the rest of us great hope. Perhaps the reason that we love Peter so much is because we identify with his humanity. Peter frequently took his eyes off of Jesus and focused instead on people or circumstances. Don't we often do the same thing?

My favorite story about Peter occurs in Matthew 14:22-31. Here we find that Peter was in a boat with the other disciples, far from shore, when a storm blew up. When they saw Jesus walking toward them on the water, they cried out in fear because they thought He was a ghost. Once they recognized Jesus, however, Peter jumped out of the boat, in obedience to Jesus' command, and began to walk toward Him on the water. Yet when he saw the wind, he felt terrified and began to sink beneath the waves. As long as he looked at Jesus, He could walk across the surface of the water, but when he began to look at his circumstances, he panicked and was overcome.

You see, mistakes don't stop God. He knows our frailties. He knows we sometimes make mistakes and stumble. The key is to learn from those mistakes and then get up and try again.

How often do we take our eyes off of Jesus when things happen that we don't understand? We allow our circumstances, our own natural inclinations and worldly deceptions to bring us down. Soon we find ourselves gripped by fear, depression and despair. But if we fix our gaze on Jesus, He will restore our hope and give us the strength to walk successfully across the deep waters of life.

Many times the Christian fails in some endeavor and tends to condemn himself. We have a habit of comparing ourselves with the people in the Bible, such as Noah and Moses. We believe because we cannot do the great exploits they did, that we are of less value than they and that we do not have a significant role in God's plan for our present age.

WAIT! Hold it a minute! You have been cheating yourself because you only compared yourself to their good works and not their human side. There are two places where all Christians are equal: First, at the foot of the cross; and the other is in human frailty. Satan loves to make us feel inferior and sadly he has great success in doing it. I want to focus in on the frailty of some of God's servants to show us how equal we really are to those in the Bible, except the Lord Jesus who never sinned.

We carry a belief that their relationship to God must have been more intimate than ours and they were super saints. This is false because we have the same relationship to God today as the Bible characters did in time past. The difference is the OT folks looked forward to the cross and we look back. Another reason I wish to focus on their failures is that if you take a step of faith and fail, your relationship with God is unaffected.

Whether we have times of success or times of failure, our relationship to God through Christ is solid and sealed.

(Eph. 4:30 KJV) "And grieve not the Holy Spirit of God, whereby ye are sealed unto the day of redemption."

Notice this verse says we are sealed! The word "sealed" means "to make fast with seal or signet, or to seal for security." The signet God sealed us with is Calvary. This means no matter how many times we fail, we are secured in Christ until the day of our redemption, which would be either our death or the return of

Christ. Of the Bible saints I mention, which one was left out of Heaven because of their failures? None!

PETER

Peter was one of Christ's most zealous servants. He was going to take the world by storm for Christ. He boasted even if all the disciples would abandon Jesus, he surely would not. Peter answered even if no one asked him a question. (Matt. 19:27; Mark 9:5) Finally, we are familiar with the fact that Peter denied Christ at the time of His betrayal. (Matt. 27:69-75) Peter was guilty of denial.

THOMAS

Thomas is widely known as "doubting Thomas" and this is an erroneous moniker. Why don't we ever say "doubting Gideon" since he put the fleece out for God to show him by sight that he was the chosen one to lead Israel. He did not believe the angel. Thomas would not believe unless he physically saw the Lord's nail prints and spear wound. We have not heard many sermons on the boldness of Thomas. In John 11:16, Thomas was willing to go back to Jerusalem with Christ, even though it would have meant his death. Thomas was guilty of unbelief. (John 20:25)

NOAH

We all know Noah built the ark on God's command, even though no rain was in sight and not due for a century. Noah obeyed resulting in the physical salvation of the human race and the animals. Noah's journey was over, the flood subsided, and they were once again on dry land, so Noah became a farmer.

One day Noah became so drunk he passed out in his tent. (Gen. 9:20-29) Noah was guilty of drunkenness.

MOSES

Moses was probably the most stressed of all God's servants having to lead about two million complaining Israelites through the desert for forty years. In Exodus 17:6, God commanded Moses to strike the rock, and when he did, fresh water gushed forth. The same scenario exists in Numbers 20:8-13. We see that God commanded Moses to just speak to the rock, but Moses, no doubt in anger and disgust, struck the rock twice with His staff in disobedience.

The symbolism here is that Christ is the rock and only once was He to be smitten as His sacrifice was the one to end all sacrifices. By Moses striking the rock again, it symbolized Christ being crucified a second time for our sins. We now speak with Christ, as Moses was supposed to speak to the rock instead of smiting it. This is a good lesson in not letting our feelings dominate our decisions. Moses was guilty of disobedience.

ELIJAH

Elijah had just experienced a great victory on Mt. Carmel, as a single representative of God. He had a part in the destruction of 450 prophets of Baal. Israel knew that God was the God of Israel, not Baal. When Queen Jezebel heard what Elijah did, she threatened him with death in twenty-four hours. Elijah ran for his life in fear of her and begged God to take his life. (1 Kings 19:3-4) Elijah was guilty of fear and faithlessness.

ABRAHAM

Abraham is known as the father of the faithful, as so plainly displayed in his willingness to sacrifice Isaac unto the Lord. We also see his faithfulness in leaving Ur of the Chaldees without a known destination. In Genesis 20 we see the story of Abraham denying the fact that Sarah was his wife because he feared Abimelech would have killed him so he could take Sarah to be his wife. Here we see the father of the faithful exhibiting great faithlessness along with dependence on human reasoning to get him out of that situation. Here we see Abraham is guilty of lying.

DAVID

David is known in Scripture as "a man after God's own heart." David did many things which pleased God. When he slew Goliath, he was the only one who saw Israel's army as the army of the living God. The rest were thinking on a physical plane. David showed great insight into spiritual matters. When David became king, he may have become prideful and believed he could do things without facing consequences for his actions. David saw Bathsheba and lusted after her. Bathsheba became pregnant so David tried to have her husband, Uriah, sleep with her so David's sin would be covered. It backfired, so David had Uriah murdered. David was guilty of lust, murder, and adultery.

These seven illustrations should serve to show us that God's choicest servants failed. Although they failed, they never lost their intimate standing before God. They enjoyed the same relationship to God the Christian does today.

I have learned that failing, while being used by God, does not negate my calling. Too many of us are stopping the forward progress we are making all because we have failed or made mistakes. Can I tell you, as long as we live in this life, we are going to make mistakes?

Another thing I want to talk with you about is making mistakes while walking in the Holy Ghost. While I do not promote experimenting on people, there are going to be times when you fall or make a mistake. I have watched my husband be a man of great prayer. I have watched as he put much emphasis on hearing from the Lord and being careful when being used by God. My husband taught me that being used by God does not mean we will not falter. We have to be careful not to use our failures as an excuse for our humanity.

Many times when people start to be used by God in the gifts of the spirit, or when we walk across the church to pray for someone, we often feel stupid and stumble. I believe theses things can be minimized if we are people of GREAT prayer. Does prayer stop failures or mistakes? No. But it does minimize the failures of walking in the spirit.

John 10:27 says, "My sheep hear my voice, and I know them, and they follow me:"

The more you pray the easier and clearer it is to hear the Master's voice. I have had many people ask me how I know I am hearing from the Lord. It is very simple. I try to talk to Him enough, that when He speaks, I KNOW it is Him. There is no mistake.

When God tells me to give someone a word, I only do exactly what my heavenly Father tells me. There are times He only speaks 3 words to me. Guess what? Those are the only 3 words I deliver. This is where wisdom comes in. My husband is blessed beyond his years with great wisdom. I trust him wholeheartedly and he has mentored me greatly. Any gift of the spirit without wisdom at its side is dangerous. It is when these types of things happen that our failures become many.

When I first started to be used by God I had a great mentor in my life; someone who was much more "hooked up" than I. This great man of God knew I was gifted with several gifts of the Spirit. He taught me to keep a journal and to write things down that the Lord spoke to me. I started to do that. I would talk with my mentor several times during the week and share with him some of my discernments and the things I felt the Lord was telling me. Some he already knew (which let me know I was hearing from the Lord) and others he said, "let's see what happens".

Sometimes, days, weeks or months later, the things I wrote down came to pass. I must have practiced this for 6 months or more before I ever stepped out and operated in the spirit. The reason for that? People were too important to me. I had been wounded by ignorant people who walked in the gifts of the spirit in the past, and there was a great fear of other people who operated like that also. So when God began to develop those things in me, I made a pact with God that if he would always allow me to be sure and hear His voice with clarity, I would treat his people with the up-most care, respect and love. From that day on, I vowed I would never speak anything unless I heard from the Lord.

There are many people that disagree with this philosophy. But most of those people are not praying people. Am I saying you will never make a mistake? No. But the mistakes should be minimal.

I had a church ask me to speak in a play one time. My lines were simple "As for me and my house we shall serve the Lord". Now I have two things I can do here. I know what they have asked me to do and say. I can do just that, or I can put my own two-cents worth in. The same goes with being used by God. It is that simple. If you only do what someone has told you to do, then you will never go wrong. What gets us into trouble is when we try to think too much on our own. When we do this, we not only open up ourselves for grave error, but we also allow the possibility of hurting the person we are ministering to. That is not worth it to me. If I only say what I have been told to say, there are fewer mistakes to make.

The answer is simple. To be used by God is a great thing. If you make a mistake, get up, brush yourself off and try again. Never, never, never stop trying.

I will never forget when my husband began to preach the Gospel. At the time I thought he was the hottest thing since fresh bread. And he was. But years later when his parents had a video and we listened to his preaching we almost cried. It was so bad we wanted to send the people he preached to an offering. Literally!

You see, never let failures stop you. Now he is one of the greatest Evangelist in our movement and powerfully used in the Gifts of the Spirit. God has a way of graduating us from one level to another. He is seeing if He can trust you. Well, can He? Sure He can. So don't give up when you fail, just get up and try again.

Part 2:

How To Keep The Anointing

Chapter Five

A Servants Heart

In order to be used by God it is imperative we have a servant's heart. A servant is simply one who serves or waits upon others. Every person I know that is highly anointed of the Lord and is now in a role of leadership, spent time somewhere as a servant and continues to have a servant's heart. However, we live in a society that tries to avoid the servant's role. We live in a dog eat dog world. Our world says "do whatever it takes to get ahead and don't worry about who you hurt in the process." Because of this, our world has become a world where taking care of me is my number one priority.

On the other hand, God expects just the opposite. God's way teaches us to bring ourselves low and then he will lift us up. His way says for me to prefer my brother. His way tells me not to be jealous when my peers are exalted, but to rejoice with them that rejoice. God's Word teaches us to wait for our appointed time and he will bring us before great men. The problem is we all hate waiting. We tend to want everything right now and in many cases, we don't want it to cost us anything in order to get it. In other words, we don't want to sacrifice anything. But sacrifice and servitude go hand in hand.

To be a servant of the Lord, there is a price to pay. When God calls you into his service there will be sacrifices that will have to be made. Sacrifice! That is another word we do not like, however, it is a great part of being a servant. Many times you will have to delay your dreams in order to assist the one you're serving to achieve their dreams. As a servant, you put the one you're serving ahead of you. You're there to make their job easier. During this season of your life there is a temptation that will come and tell you you're ready to do things on your own. It is important that you stay under the covering of those over you. God in due season will exalt you. I'm reminded of the story of Elisha in I Kings 19:19-21. There are several things that stand out to me in this story.

The first thing is Elisha was in a servant's role when the man of God found him. Even though he had servants under him, he was not above putting his hand to the plow. Why? He was still submitted to his father and was busy serving him. The Bible says that Elijah "found Elisha". When you're a servant that is faithful, God will make sure you're discovered. It is important for you to grow where you are planted. In other words, wherever you are at, become a servant and remain faithful to those you are serving. As you grow and the time is right, God will make room for you in new areas of ministry.

The second thing that stands out to me in this story is Elisha was working. He was busy. He was active. In my travels, I meet people all the time that are waiting for a position of ministry to open up to them, but they are not doing anything in the mean time. I have a problem with a minister that never ministers. You do not need to be told to minister. A true minister will have a servant's heart and find a way to serve. You will never be discovered by God or man until you get active serving in some capacity or another. Notice the men Jesus chose to be his disciples. Some were busy fishing, others tax collecting. Luke was a physician. God never calls lazy people. He always calls people who are willing to put their hand to the plow.

The next thing that happened was the man of God came and cast his mantle upon Elisha. Now he was being invited into a new level of servitude. I find it interesting that Elisha was not looking for the promotion but that the promotion found him. Elijah, by casting his mantle upon Elisha, was saying come under my covering and be my servant. Elisha was not begged or coheresed but simply invited. When Elisha wanted to go and tell his parents good-bye, the man of God did not forbid him. The man of God knew that if this was to be then Elisha would return and serve him. And return he did. The Bible says that Elisha "ministered unto him". In Matthew Henry's Commentary he writes that Elisha "ministered to him as his servitor, poured water on his hands, (2 Kin. 3:11). It is of great advantage to young ministers to spend some time under the direction of those that are aged and experienced, whose years teach wisdom, and not to think much, if occasion be, to minister to them. Those that would be fit to teach must have time to learn; and those that hope hereafter to rise and rule must be willing at first to stoop and serve." (from Matthew Henry's Commentary)

I was invited to minister in a church in Oklahoma several years ago. This church was not affiliated with my organization of ministry, so for me to get an invitation to minister there meant God was up to something. The church was small and nobody I knew had ever heard of it. It was here, however, I met a young man that had a servant's heart. This man was busy working for the Lord. Whatever the church or pastor needed, this man was there to do it. He played the piano, he helped lead the services, and he helped the young people. He would even buy broken down cars, fix them, and then sell the cars and give the money to the church so they could have their camp meeting. This servant and I made a connection in the spirit. I knew from that time on that God would do great things in this man's life. We stayed in touch from time to time over the next few years. There were several times he became frustrated and wanted to give up, but he had a servant's heart and just kept giving.

I was ministering in a great church that ran around 400 or 500 people in Louisiana. The pastor there told me he was looking for someone to assist him. I immediately thought of my friend from Oklahoma. With a few phone calls and a few visits this guy became the assistant pastor of this great church. My friend still has the heart of a servant and is busier than ever working for the Lord. One day he will be discovered again and become pastor of another great church. We still talk about how amazing God is when we think about how God put us together in that little town in Oklahoma.

Juanita Bynum, in her book "My Spiritual Inheritance" said, "When you obey, you are complying with someone else's wishes or orders. You are acknowledging someone else's authority. God perfectly designed the plan of salvation through Jesus when He said, "No man cometh unto the Father, but by me" (John 14:6, KJV). We can't ignore earthly authority and think we're going to reach the Father. How can we? God designed His plan so that we would walk in spiritual order."[ii]

Too many people want the anointing with no strings attached. I have learned though, that the greatest of my anointing developed while under the strict direction of spiritual leadership. It is not what the flatterers say about me that matters as much as those who really know me.

Bynum went on to say, "You will never go to your next level until you are willing to give up those who think you are wonderful in order to stand in the presence of somebody who can discern the areas that you are awful in."[iii]

"The point is, if God can't trust your character enough to "take" a shot (from your leaders) as an arrow of deliverance, He certainly can't trust you to "give" a shot to someone else. When you are in a battle, and you are in the ring, you have to be able to take a blow in order to give a blow. And what you take, what you're willing to let leadership impart into you, will only testify of the level that you will be able to impart. You must understand that the most important factor is for you to remain in the right atmosphere, in the company of those who can usher you to your next level."[iv]

"When Timothy was concerned about his age, Paul told him, "When I call to remembrance the unfeigned faith that is in thee, which dwelt first in thy grandmother Lois and thy mother Eunice; and am persuaded that in thee also. Wherefore I put thee in remembrance that thou stir up the gift of God, which is in thee by the putting on of my hands" (2 Tim. 1:5-6, KJV). Timothy didn't have an anointing on his own; it was given to him through the spiritual DNA of his mother and grandmother, and by the laying on of Paul's hands it was activated.

I said this earlier, but it bears repeating here. Understand that when God uses a man or woman of God to place an anointing upon you, the next step of receiving that anointing is to come under submission. The anointing in you must be channeled and guided. It must be placed under great counsel, because you are wearing something that you are unfamiliar with. And though it may feel good that the mighty hand of God is resting upon you, one fact remains-you haven't been trained to operate effectively in that particular anointing or gift."[v]

It seems to me that Christians are the only ones who don't want to be accountable or coached by anyone. In essence, what we are saying is, I view my own knowledge and experience so highly, I don't need anyone else, especially when they go against what I think, say, or do. The ultimate way to great things in God, is first, submitting ourselves to spiritual authority. Sound spiritual counsel is a safety net to those who are growing in grace.

At all cost we must keep a servants heart. While serving in the ministry, I am reminded that to be a servant is to be the greatest leader of all. Bishop L.A. Parents' wife was on her death bed when several people went to visit her. One of her last statements gripped my heart very powerfully. She said, "you know dear, we have missed it in ministry these days. Papa and I were servants to the people and we constantly went out of our way to be there for them and serve them. Now day's ministry is just the opposite. It is all about serving the ministry instead of ministry serving the people.

Am I saying we shouldn't serve the ministry? No, that is not what I'm saying. We should most assuredly serve the ministry with our best efforts. But ministry must be the leader at all times, and to do that means the leader must be the greatest servant of all.

I am reminded of the story when Laban and Jacob decided to go their separate ways. In doing this, Laban wanted to give Jacob an inheritance, or wages for his work. Jacob said, "I don't want anything. But he ask if he could have the brown, speckled, spotted sheep and goats. Laban agreed to do so. I want you to read here what Jacob does next:

Genesis 30:30-43 reads;

> "For it was little which thou hadst before I came, and it is now increased unto a multitude; and the LORD hath blessed thee since my coming: and now when shall I provide for mine own house also?
>
> And he said, What shall I give thee? And Jacob said, Thou shalt not give me any thing: if thou wilt do this thing for me, I will again feed and keep thy flock.
>
> I will pass through all thy flock to day, removing from thence all the speckled and spotted cattle, and all the brown cattle among the sheep, and the spotted and speckled among the goats: and of such shall be my hire.
>
> So shall my righteousness answer for me in time to come, when it shall come for my hire before thy face: every one that is not speckled and spotted among the goats, and brown among the sheep, that shall be counted stolen with me.
>
> And Laban said, Behold, I would it might be according to thy word.
>
> And he removed that day the he goats that were ringstraked and spotted, and all the she goats that were speckled and spotted, and every one that had some white in it, and all the brown among the sheep, and gave them into the hand of his sons.

And he set three days' journey betwixt himself and Jacob: and Jacob fed the rest of Laban's flocks.

And Jacob took him rods of green poplar, and of the hazel and chestnut tree; and pilled white strakes in them, and made the white appear which was in the rods.

And he set the rods which he had pilled before the flocks in the gutters in the watering troughs when the flocks came to drink, that they should conceive when they came to drink.

And the flocks conceived before the rods, and brought forth cattle ringstraked, speckled, and spotted.

And Jacob did separate the lambs, and set the faces of the flocks toward the ringstraked, and all the brown in the flock of Laban; and he put his own flocks by themselves, and put them not unto Laban's cattle.

And it came to pass, whensoever the stronger cattle did conceive, that Jacob laid the rods before the eyes of the cattle in the gutters, that they might conceive among the rods.

But when the cattle were feeble, he put them not in: so the feebler were Laban's, and the stronger Jacob's.

And the man increased exceedingly, and had much cattle, and maidservants, and menservants, and camels, and asses."

Jacob took the sheep, goats and stripped rods, then set the stripped rods in the sight of the sheep and goat as they came to drink. When the animals saw the stripped rods, they produced spotted and stripped offspring.

You see, you become what you sit under and what you see. Some of you are wondering why you are the way you are and why you are producing some things in your life. My question to you is, "What are you looking at? What is getting in your spirit as you drink and eat?" It goes back to the same principal of sowing and reaping. What you put in is going to come out. It is important to surround yourself with other great leaders. Having a spiritual father that can see farther than you is an invaluable asset in order to be mentored in the ways of the spirit. Keeping a servants heart can keep you from tremendous failures and pitfalls.

I know some of you feel like you are never going to arrive, but let me encourage you to hold on. There will be a time that God graduates you from being a servant to being a leader. Rest assured when God gets ready it will happen. Only God lifts up and brings low. If you are not being elevated it is because you are not ready yet.

If you will keep a servants heart God will make sure you are discovered. I'm reminded of the story of David and Saul. Saul began to be troubled by an evil spirit. Saul said, find me a man that can play a harp well. One of Saul's servants said, I have seen a man; one of the sons of Jesse named David. David was called from tending sheep to come and play his harp for a king. He went from sleeping with sheep in the wilderness to sleeping in the palace of the king over night. All of it happened because God made sure he was noticed by the right person at the right time.

Don't be discouraged! God has not forgotten you. There are people watching you right now. They see your sacrifice and your labor of love. God will make sure they remember you at the appointed time. You shall reap in due season if you faint not. Most of all, be God's greatest servant of all.

Chapter Six

To Succeed, You Must Pass the Test

"Love Not the World, neither the things that are in the world...." I John 2:15

We have to be very careful how much we love the world. Samson never fell until he gave his heart to Delilah. He slept with a whore at Gahaza, and still kept his anointing. But when it came to Delilah, the Bible said, "He loved her, and told her all his heart." Whatever your heart is attached to can become an opportunity to zap your strength. The Bible said, "love not the world, neither the things that are in the world, for he that has the love of the world, the love of the father is not in him." Then it goes on to say "All that is in the world, is the lust of the flesh, the lust of the eye, and the pride of life." (1 John 2:16)

We can put every test of life into **3 phases**: the **lust of the flesh**, the **lust of the eyes**, and the **pride of life**. These 3 things are the paramount things that trouble us.

Hebrews 4:15

> "For we have not an high priest which cannot be touched with the feeling of our infirmities; but was in all **points** tempted like as we are, yet without sin."

Christ was tempted with all points. What is the difference between the specificity of sin and the points of sin? We evaluate sin by specificity. We condemn some for doing one thing, while we are sinning in another area. There are acceptable and non-acceptable sins as far as we are concerned.

We often preach the hardest on the things we didn't do, and have the most compassion for the things we did do. This causes people to become confused.

The scripture said there are only three points to be tempted in. The details don't matter. That's why you are foolish to tell people the details about your life. Always generalize. Don't be too specific. People love the details, but God just looks at the points. If anyone knew what it was to be tested, Jesus did. He was tempted in all points.

We can put every test of life into **three phases**:

- **Lust of the flesh.**

- **Lust of the eyes.**

- **Pride of life.**

These three things are the paramount things that trouble us.

God is not into details; he is into points. Man looks on the outward, but God looks on the heart.

We fight the enemy in one of these three areas. The devil only has three weapons. And if you can overcome these three things, then "no weapon formed against you can prosper." (Isaiah 54:17)

The only weapons the enemy can use are:

- **Lust of the flesh.**

- **Lust of the eyes.**

- **Pride of life.**

No matter what you are struggling with, every sin falls within one of these three categories.

It's something your flesh is craving, something your eye saw, or some attitude you have in your heart. If you can overcome your flesh, get singleness of eye, and purge your heart, then the devil is out of ammunition.

When sin was ready to enter the world, it came in three points. It all started in the garden. You'll notice that God never told us what the fruit was because God doesn't care about details. He is only interested in points.

Genesis 3:6

> "And when the woman saw that the tree was good for food, and that it was pleasant to the eyes, and a tree to be desired to make one wise, she took of the fruit thereof, and did eat, and gave also unto her husband with her; and he did eat."

If Eve could have overcome those three things, sin would have never entered the world. There were three tests:

- What her flesh craved.

- What her eye saw.

- The secret longings of her heart.

Those three things led to her demise. When she saw that it was pleasant to the eye, that it was good for food, and it was desirous to make one wise, she took the fruit. When Eve gave to man, he fell in three points: the lust of the flesh, the lust of the eyes, and the pride of life.

If he never had taken the fruit, he would have had the option of doing what the second man Adam had. The second man

Adam died for his bride. The first man Adam died with his bride.

All humanity fell behind three points. Generational curses fell behind three points.

That is why it is important to set the standard right now. If you are going to be anointed, you are going to be tested in three areas of your life. There will not only be three tests in your life, but tests will come in cycles until you die. And that's good, because what would it be like to pass the test once and never have to try again. God made it where you will have to pass three tests every time He takes you to a new level in the Spirit.

I want to tell all of you who are anointed and waiting for your time, God is about to call you out.

Some people are trying to accomplish things they have not been pointed out to do. You may be anointed, but you will have to wait until you are appointed before you walk into the fullness of your anointing. Being anointed is not enough. You must wait until you are appointed.

John points out Jesus and says, "Behold the Lamb of God which taketh away the sins of the world." When that happened, He went from obscurity to notoriety. From being a no-name to having a name exalted above every name. From being a face in the crowd to being the one everyone was looking for.

God will not endorse you if you rebel against leadership. We need to clean some of this junk out of the church. We have too many renegades, and too much rebellion. There are too many strange spirits in the church. People are doing what is right in their own eyes. If you are not appointed, being anointed will not be enough.

Even Jesus had to pass the three tests.

Matthew 4:1-3

> Then was Jesus led up of the Spirit into the wilderness to be tempted of the devil.
>
> And when he had fasted forty days and forty nights, he was afterward an hungered.
>
> And when the tempter came to him, he said, If thou be the Son of God, command that these stones be made bread.
>
> But he answered and said, It is written, Man shall not live by bread alone, but by every word that proceedeth out of the mouth of God.
>
> Then the devil taketh him up into the holy city, and setteth him on a pinnacle of the temple,
>
> And saith unto him, If thou be the Son of God, cast thyself down: for it is written, He shall give his angels charge concerning thee: and in their hands they shall bear thee up, lest at any time thou dash thy foot against a stone.

Jesus said unto him, It is written again, Thou shalt not tempt the Lord thy God.

Again, the devil taketh him up into an exceeding high mountain, and sheweth him all the kingdoms of the world, and the glory of them;

And saith unto him, All these things will I give thee, if thou wilt fall down and worship me.

Then saith Jesus unto him, Get thee hence, Satan: for it is written, Thou shalt worship the Lord thy God, and him only shalt thou serve.

The **first test** he had to face was; **"If thou be the Son of God, command that these stones be made bread."**

This is nothing but the **lust of the flesh**. Your hunger is not wrong, but it's how you satisfy your hunger that is wrong. The hunger is divine, but how you satisfy it may be corrupt. God put the passion in your body, but you can't feed yourself anywhere you want to. There is nothing wrong with flesh; it's the Lust of the flesh that's getting us into trouble.

What is awesome here is Jesus defeated him with the Word. What you need is more Word.

The **second test** he had to face was; **"Again, the devil taketh him up into an exceeding high mountain, and sheweth him all the kingdoms of the world, and the glory of them; And saith unto him, All these things will I give thee, if thou wilt fall down and worship me".**

This was the lust of the eye. You've got to watch what you see. You've got to protect yourself from what you look at. When I started driving I learned that if I looked off the road my car would go in the direction of my vision. You've got to keep your eyes on the road.

The **third test** He had to face was; "Then the devil taketh him up into the holy city, and setteth him on a pinnacle of the temple, And saith unto him, If thou be the Son of God, cast thyself down: for it is written, He shall give his angels charge concerning thee: and in their hands they shall bear thee up, lest at any time thou dash thy foot against a stone." Matt 4:5-6.

The pride of life is the pressure to perform and the need to impress those around us. It is the need to prove to others who you really are: the need for human validation. It is all the pride of life.

The church has preached against the lust of the flesh, and the lust of the eye, but we have said very little about "The Pride of Life." I have to say that I am a little concerned, because the pride of life is the most dangerous of the three. I want to remind you that the Bible said there are three things that the Lord hates. And the third thing is always the strongest dimension.

Now abideth (1) Faith, (2) Hope & (3) Charity, but the greatest of these is Charity. (The third thing)

(1) The Outer Court (2) The Inner Court and (3) the Holies of Holies. The greatest is the Holies of Holies.

(1) Body (2) Soul and (3) Spirit, (The greatest is the Spirit).

Whenever there are three, the third is always the greatest dimension.

- The lust of the flesh
- The lust of the eyes
- The pride of life.

I heard T.D. Jakes once say, "I asked God, if we are living in the last days, then why is the enemy treating the church so nice? God said, "The enemy hasn't gotten soft, He has moved from natural martyrs to spiritual martyrs."

When the early church was persecuted, they were stoned. We get upset when someone talks about us. Paul would have laughed us right out of the church. Our idea of persecution is fighting people on our job. We are spoiled. That's our problem. Some of us haven't been through enough to complain about. This is the third dimension. It is the pride of life.

I have never seen it like I have in the church today: the pressure to perform. Everyone is jockeying for position. Struggling to get up and be seen. We try to be recognized and fight for our own turf. This is a spirit. It is spiritual warfare. It is the pride of life.

You can get anyone to sit up front, but you can't get anyone to clean the floors in the church. We want the Lord to use us but only in high, visible positions. This is the pride of life. People are leaving churches because they want to go somewhere where they can be used. When in reality, it is not that they want to be used, as much as they want to be seen.

Pride is the secret weapon of the enemy coming against the church to destroy it. It is a sign that the end is coming. The Bible says that "Pride cometh before a fall." The very fact that the spirit of pride is taking over the church is a sign that we are about to come to the end of time. The closer we get to the end of time, the more people are going to feel the pressure to be like those around us. What you really need to do is be yourself.

Some of you are jockeying for things you didn't need, only to find out that what you wanted is not what you got. It was the pride of life that led us to these places. Why haven't we preached harder against pride?

God made a list of the seven things that He hates. The sin He hated the most was not adultery, it was not lust, and it wasn't backbiting. It was pride. God hates pride so much He even hates the look of pride. "He said a proud look I despise." (Proverbs 6:17) He despises uppity looking people full of arrogance and self-reliance.

Some of us have forgotten where we came from. How can we come into church with our nose in the air, when a few years ago God pulled you out of perversion and all kinds of hell? I'll tell you how. We have forgotten who we were and where God has brought us from. Sometimes I wish that God could put up a screen in our churches and scan the minds of His people, and show everyone what is going through our minds. Then some of us would be more careful about what our minds are entertaining.

I have learned that we all have struggles. It's the pride of life that tries to cover up these struggles. I'm not saying we need to reveal all that is going on and what we've done in our lives. That might really scare some of you. But I do believe we need to be a people of a meek and lowly spirit reflecting the heavenly Father at all times.

The pride of life is wrecking marriages, ministries, and minds. Some folks sit around mad saying, "When is God going to use me"? I'll tell you when God is going to use you, when He can trust you. It's not your business to be used; it is your business to be available. God uses whomever He wants to. But the pride of life will cause you to see yourself in a light that is not godly. It is called the pride of life.

If you don't get rid of pride it will defile you. It will corrupt you. The Bible says that "If you exalt yourself, God would abase you, but if you humble yourself God would exalt you." (Job 40:11) That's why in the Bible, every time you saw God blessing a man or a woman, they fell on their face. The way to get blessed was to go down. The lower you get, the higher God will take you.

We're too high to be blessed. We're too arrogant to be blessed. He said to humble yourself and God would exalt you. It's time to be blessed. If you don't get your blessing, it will be because of the pride of life. The problem with church folks is some think they have to make it happen. You don't have to make it happen. When God gets ready to bless you, no man will be able to stop it. You don't have to make it happen. You just need to let it happen. I'm telling you to let it happen. Take your hands off God and let it happen.

The enemy doesn't want this message to get out. There are too many folks around you that are carnal. They are so fleshly they are making you spiritually sick.

Some of you need to start praying and quit talking. The enemy is gassing us with our pride and our need to show off. We need to humble ourselves and turn our face to Him again. I know that some of you want to be used by God in a greater measure. I am telling you in order to do so, we are going to have to take this old flesh back to an altar and submit ourselves one more time to the Spirit of God and seek His face, His agenda and His purpose. When we do, that is when the church is going to spring forth in her greatest hour.

Cleanse us Jesus. Cleanse our thoughts. Cleanse our mind. Cleanse our heart. Cleanse our motives. Cleanse our tongue. Cleanse how we talk. Cleanse how we say things. Cleanse us Holy Spirit. For we know we can pass these three tests.

Chapter Seven

Contagious

Contagious; Webster's Dictionary defines Contagious as: Communicable as by contact; to convey from one to another; spreading among many.

The early church was contagious. They were filled with such passion; everyone they came in contact with was changed in some form or fashion. The early church was, without doubt, full of the fire of the Holy Ghost.

Acts 4:7 says, "And when they had set them in the midst, they asked, by what power, or by what name, have ye done this? Then Peter, filled with the Holy Ghost, said unto them, Ye rulers of the people and elders of Israel, If we this day be examined of the good deed done to the impotent man, by what means he is made whole; Be it known unto you all, and to all the people of Israel, that by the name of Jesus Christ of Nazareth, whom ye crucified, whom God raised from the dead, even by him doth this man stand here before you whole. This is the stone which was set at naught of you builders, which is become the head of the corner. Neither is their salvation in any other: for there is none other name under heaven given among men, whereby we must be saved. Now when they saw the boldness of Peter and John, and perceived that they were unlearned and ignorant men, they marveled; and they took knowledge of them, that they had been with Jesus."

Drop down to verse 17: "But that is spread no further among the people, let us straitly threaten them, that they speak henceforth to no man in this name. And they called them, and commanded them not to speak at all nor teach in the name of Jesus. But Peter and John answer and said unto them, Whether it be right in the sight of God to hearken unto you more than unto God, judge ye. For we can not but speak the things which we have seen and heard."

The early believers were analyzed by the high priest Annas, and critiqued by Caiaphas, because they could not explain the phenomenon of this tremendous transformation that had taken place in the lives of this people. Their perception concluded they did not get this out of a classroom. For they said these are unlearned and ignorant men. Yet there was a boldness and assertiveness about these Apostolic's that defied logic, but could not be denied.

The reason for their remarkable change is found in verse 8. Where the scripture simply states, "Then Peter full of the Holy Ghost..."

He didn't get this in a classroom. He didn't get this in a University. He got this when he was filled with the Holy Ghost.

The word "filled" in that particular verse is a very picturesque word. It is the same word that is found in the scriptures, when it describes the nets that were filled with fish until they could hold no more. It is the same word that is used at other times to describe a piece of cloth that is soaked in die, until every strand and fiber in the fabric has been altered by the application.

The church was a radical proposal that was more than remodeled Judaism, but it was a new concept that Jesus described as "new wine" in new wine skins. It was too potent. It was too powerful to be contained in the old covenant.

The contents of this new experience would be manifested through the lives of the Lords' church and it would include: signs, wonders and miracles.

The supernatural and the unexplainable would be demonstrated by these disciples. There is no other explanation for this extraordinary growth of the early church. Then there was a new life form that was unseen to the natural eye, that had been let loose in the Upper Room. It was threatening to sweep the world.

Most of us believe experientially, that we've got the same Holy Ghost that they had in the old times in the book of Acts?

Yet, I believe the early church might have had something that I wish somehow would get a hold of us last day Apostolics. I'm convinced that is the key that will propel us into the last day move of God.

I believe the early church, the grass roots level of the early church, the everyday believer in the early church was not just a hero here and there. The grass roots believer of the early church walked in an awareness and was cognoscente of the presence and the power of God that was coursing through them.

I want you to know there was an awareness inside of them of the power and the dynamic of the Spirit of the Almighty God.

I am convinced of this fact when I read in Acts chapter 19 that diseases were cured and devils were cast out when they brought handkerchiefs and aprons from the body of the Apostle Paul and laid them upon sick folk. Devils fled and diseases got out of there. Why? Because there was something dynamic, awesome and powerful about what the Sprit of God could do through those believers.

When the Apostle Paul had to give explanation concerning his miracle ministry, we find his explanation simply given in Galatians 2:20. He said, "Christ liveth in me." This is not me.

If it was me it would be enticing words of mens' wisdom, but it's not me. It's Christ liveth in me."

This kind of unique awareness was not just among a few heroes of that early church but in the grass roots among the believers. They walked everyday in that awareness. It was still upon their ears the words of Jesus, "I am with you, but I shall be in you."

What would happen? What would take place if God's people, not just the preachers, not just the preachers' wife's, but every saint of God, every tongue talker, every person baptized in Jesus name could walk in the power and the demonstration of the Holy Ghost?

I'll tell you what would happen. We would have the kind of revival that God wants to visit upon the Church of the Most High God.

Somebody said the modern church has more fashion than passion; more pathetic than prophetic; more superficial than supernatural. They traded in their prayer meetings for ice cream socials; their Bible Studies for ladies teas and revivals for chicken dinners, and that is why they are as cold as the ice cream as weak as the tea and as dead as the chicken.

My God doesn't want a dead church. <u>My God wants a people that know what's on the inside of them</u>. My God wants a church that knows the power of God that dwells inside of them.

We are in the last days and we're still the answer for this generation.

The truth of the matter is God has set the stage for an unprecedented move of the Spirit. There has got to be someone that takes advantage of this opportunity. There has to be someone that says this is not just an accident. We are here by Divine decree and God has his hand upon this church.

We are not going to reach our world by clapping, and we are not going to reach our world by waiving our hands. We have got to know what is on the inside of us. We have got to know the Power of God that dwells within us.

This revival is not going to be accomplished by technique but touch. Not by programs but by people. That is not a slap against the programs of the Church. We have got some wonderful dynamic programs, but if we are relying on our programs to touch this generation the way they need to be touched, programs by themselves are dead and lifeless.

Someone has to pick up these programs with the power of God inside of them. Someone has to implement these things with the Holy Ghost and fire. God has endued you with a power that is contagious.

We can all have revival if we mobilize our people to believe that we can individually make a difference.

In the book of Acts I see them converting the world, house to house, heart to heart, and not waiting to call in some evangelist, but knowing and being cognoscente of what was on the inside of them.

The Aids virus has been traced to the interior of Africa, to possibly one man that was infected by a Chimpanzee. From that one person this epidemic has caused the death of 22 million people and another 36 million people are infected with the virus. That totals 58 million people; all because one man was contagious.

If death can do it, so can life. If tragedy can do it, so can truth. . If sin can do it, so can salvation.

You are contagious. You are a walking revival. You are a walking move of God. The power of God that resides in you is phenomenal. It is fantastic.

As I began to study the early church and the great revival meetings they had, they all had one thing in common. They were extremely contagious. The more I thought about this I began to do some studying on what caused someone to be contagious. FEVER; Fever causes a person to become contagious. My question to you is; Are you contagious? Are you running a fever? If not, I question how contagious you are.

Fevers are defined as temperatures being over 100 °F. The body temperature is normally 98.6 °F or 37 °C, and is regulated by the body's own temperature -control systems.

You will not need treatment unless your temperature rises over 102 °F or 39 °C. If this happens, you may look flushed, refuse to eat and drink or cry a lot. A fever is likely to be caused by an underlying infection.

If you have a mildly raised temperature which is not above 101°F or 38.5°C and you are alert, eating, drinking and playing normally, then there's no need to start heading for the doctor. Wait to see if your temperature goes up or down before taking any further action.

What kind of fever are your running? Are you hot to the touch or are you a lukewarm Christian? We must be infected with the power of the Holy Ghost to the point where our actions and our appetites become completely affected by this fever called the "Holy Ghost". A real Holy Ghost fever will cause your appetite to change from worldly things to spiritual things. A real fever will cause you to cry in prayer and seek the face of God. A real fever will cause you to feel flushed! We must be a changing agent in this world.

Because we are infected with fever from on high, the enemy is doing everything he can to stop that. When a normal fever is in the physical body, this is what must be done to bring it down:

If you have a temperature of over 102°F or 39°C, you are suffering from fever and need urgent care. You can help by following these instructions quickly to help bring the temperature down: keep yourself and the room you are in cool, even if you are shivering. If you have a temperature of over 101°F or 38.5°C, you can also help to bring the temperature down by sponging with lukewarm water.

Doesn't that sound like what the enemy is prescribing for the Church? Keep us cold. Keep our churches cold and make sure we are affected by lukewarm water. If that doesn't sound like what the enemy is trying to do in this end time move of the spirit

I am not sure what it is. The enemy is doing everything he can to try and keep us from being contagious. But the devil is a liar.

Understand you were called to be a contagious Christian. The doctor will tell you to keep a child indoors if he or she is running a fever. If a fever is present then that person is very contagious. I want to be a contagious Christian with a high fever. I want to affect everything around me.

What about you? Are you contagious? Are your running a fever? If not, check your temperature and see what the underlying cause is. Is it Luke warmness or are you infected with the things of this world. Get on fire for God and know you have been called to be contagious. Let's get the fever for revival!!

Bibliography

Chapter Four

[i] Dr. Yongi Cho, (pgs. 36-50 – The Fourth Dimension)

Chapter Five

[ii] My Spiritual Inheritance, Juanita Bynum, Pg. 29
[iii] Ibid, Pg. 59
[iv] Ibid, Pg. 67
[v] Ibid, Pg. 78

Chapter Six

Inspired by T.D. Jakes in a public message called, "The Pride of Life."

Chapter Seven

Part of this chapter was taken from General Conference, 2001, Rev. Terry Cox's message "Watch out ! I'm contagious". W/Permission

Books by Shirley Carson, D.R.E.
Book Order Form

To order books:

1. Fill out the hard copy of the order form.
2. Enclose a check or money order in US dollars for the books ordered.
3. Mail payment and completed form to us at the address below.

Name_____

Street Address_____

City_____

State_____

Zip Code_____

_____ What Do You See In The Flame? - $10.00

_____ Women Of Warfare - $10.00

_____ God Still Heals - $10.00

_____ The Criss Cross Blessing - $10.00

_____ So You Want To Be Used By God? - $10.00

Shipping: add $3.00 *per order*

Total enclosed: $_____

Mail order form along with check or money order made payable to:

Shirley Carson   Contact # 337-356-9156
4050 Silver Valley Dr.
Orion, Michigan 48359